Greenhill Books

MACHINE-GUNS OF
TWO WORLD WARS

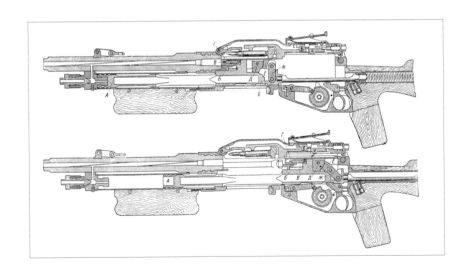

GREENHILL MILITARY MANUALS

A German gun crew with an MG.13 (Dreyse), pictured in the early 1930s during the Reichwehr period.

MACHINE-GUNS OF TWO WORLD WARS

GREENHILL MILITARY MANUALS

John Walter

Greenhill Books, London
Stackpole Books, Pennsylvania

Greenhill Books

To ARW and ADW, for keeping me relatively sane during work on this book . . .

Machine-guns of Two World Wars
first published 2005 by
Greenhill Books, Lionel Leventhal Limited, Park House, 1 Russell Gardens, London NW11 9NN
www.greenhillbooks.com
and
Stackpole Books, 5067 Ritter Road, Mechanicsburg, PA 17055, USA

British Library Cataloguing in Publication Data
Walter, John
Machine guns of two world wars
1. Machine guns – History
2. World War, 1939–1945 – Equipment
I. Title
623.4'424

ISBN 1-85367-606-3

Library of Congress Cataloging-in-Publication Data available

Designed by John Anastasio

Printed and bound in Singapore

Contents

Acknowledgements

This book is effectively a 'prequel' to Modern Machine-guns, published in the Military Manuals series in 2000. At the time the original book was written, Machine-guns of Two World Wars was not being considered. Consequently, the historical introduction that rightly belongs here instead occupies the first few pages of Modern Machine-guns. In the introduction that follows, therefore, I have tried to concentrate on the development of the machine-gun from technological and tactical viewpoints instead of history!

This has kept duplication to a minimum. However, the service careers of guns such as the 0.50 Browning (or the German MG. 42, in its MG3 guise) have lasted until the present day, and so a limited overlap between the two books is unavoidable.

The illustrations have been supplied from a number of sources, but I would particularly like to acknowledge the debt I owe to Ian Hogg, who sadly died in March 2002. Ian cheerfully supplied me with many photographs, drawings and snippets of information over the years we knew each other, and I miss his contributions greatly.

I would also like to acknowledge the help given by Christian Cranmer and Fire-Power International Ltd, who supplied some of the photographs – particularly of the German/Turkish MG. 08 – and Vickers Ltd, for pictures of the Vickers-Berthier, Vickers 'D' and Vickers 'K' guns.

Compiling this book reminded me not only that there is still much to learn about this particular subject, but also that many of the published sources are contradictory. Many English-language books still repeat information taken from books such as Small Arms of the World, (originally dating from the 1940s) or even Military Small Arms of the Twentieth Century (with origins in the early 1970s), and seem to pay little attention to work that has since been undertaken in countries such as France and Germany. I have tried to check as many individual details as possible and the source of information is given with each data table. But I would still be interested to learn of anything that should be altered for a future edition, and recognise that, ultimately, the responsibility for mistakes is mine alone.

John Walter, Hove, 2005

Introduction

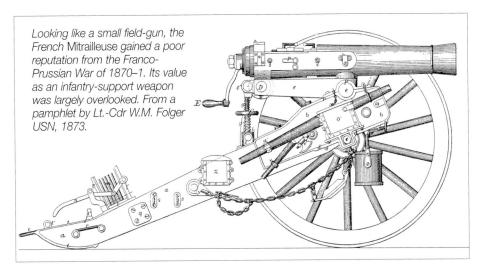

Looking like a small field-gun, the French Mitrailleuse *gained a poor reputation from the Franco-Prussian War of 1870–1. Its value as an infantry-support weapon was largely overlooked. From a pamphlet by Lt.-Cdr W.M. Folger USN, 1873.*

Though mechanically-operated machine-guns such as the Gatling, the Gardner and Nordenfelt had seen action during the last quarter of the nineteenth century – often to good effect – the advent of the Maxim signified that their day had ended. Though some US Army Gatlings were still on the army inventory as late as 1915, self-actuation removed the physical strain of sustaining fire for long periods.

However, even the Maxim, which was an exceptionally efficient weapon, took time to perfect and the transition from manual to automatic operation was not instant. Many armies looked askance at the new designs, failing totally to comprehend their value, and were reluctant to commit to re-equipment. Much has been written concerning the conservatism of army authorities, especially when attempting to apportion blame for the slaughter of the First World War, and a key factor was undoubtedly the promotion to high rank of far too

many cavalrymen – the self-professed elite of the army. Yet it is difficult to be truly objective a century after the events.

The Russo-Japanese War of 1904–5 was the first in which 'automatic' machine-guns were used in quantity, though the numbers were not large enough to impinge either on public opinion (the Battle of Tsushima and the Siege of Port Arthur made much more interesting reading) or the military establishment. The lessons had been clear to those who were prepared to retain an open mind, though the tactical use of the Russian Maxims and Madsens against the Japanese Hotchkiss guns still posed as many questions as it answered.

Many armies simply ignored the implications. There were several reasons for this lax and ultimate costly attitude. Though the machine-gun had been brought to a satisfactory state of perfection, the guns were expensive and complicated. They performed well enough in the hands of trained men – though rarely as well as they did in trials – but had proved vulnerable to counter-attack. Some observers worried that they could be as easily turned against their erstwhile owners, creating an obsession not so much with battlefield mobility but

British sailors man a Maxim Gun on a wheeled mount, from a picture published in the Army & Navy Illustrated *in August 1896.*

increased vulnerability to counter-fire by raising the bore-line far too far from ground level.

The French had made mistakes of this type with the Mitrailleuse during the Franco-Prussian War, even though the primitive machine-guns had shown their value when used as close-range infantry support, but many people were still following the same tack as late as 1914. Some armies had formed special infantry-support units, usually in the form of independent machine-gun companies, but effectiveness was restricted by the small numbers of guns that were purchased. The First World War was to show that maximum 'fire density', which meant quantity (if necessary at the expense of quality), was the most important criterion.

Reliability was another diverting sideshow. The Maxims and the Hotchkiss guns had performed reliably during the Russo-Japanese War, but the Madsens, brought into service only at the end of hostilities, were prone to jamming. Consequently, though the Russians retained the Maxim after the war had ended, the Madsens were discarded. That this was partly due to internal politics – the Russian army authorities blamed much of their defeat on the cowardice of the cavalry – was not obvious to Western observers, and the lesson was assumed to be that only heavyweight machine-guns had a future.

more on the ease with which machine-guns could be withdrawn from the battlefield if threatened.

The result initially was to confine machine-guns to fortresses, strong-points and similar defensive positions, or to regard them as light artillery. This created the need for cumbersome wheeled carriages, often requiring the services of two or more horses to move them, and

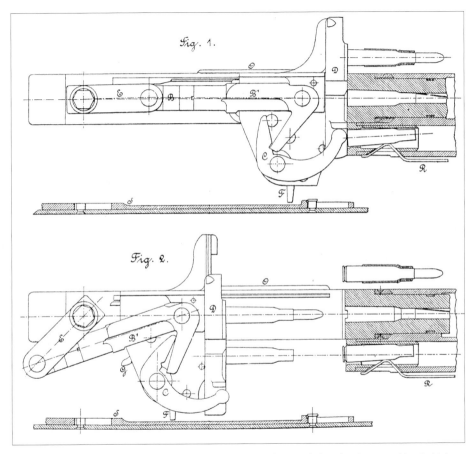

The basic mechanism of the Maxim gun, showing how the toggle breaks down and back. Note also how the feed-slide moves vertically to present a new round to the chamber. From Braun's Das Maxim-Maschinengewehr und seine Verwendung *(1905).*

But the Maxims were recoil-operated and water-cooled, whereas the Hotchkiss was gas-operated and air cooled.

There is no doubt that the Hotchkiss was much simpler than the Maxim, but trials showed that it was incapable of sustaining fire for lengthy periods. Even though the barrel was fitted with radiator fins, it rapidly heated to a point where bullets no longer engaged in the rifling and, ultimately, the bore was ruined. Most water-cooled guns could fire tens of thousands of rounds without stopping.

When the First World War began, few of the participants had extensive inventories of machine-guns and only a few manufacturers – Vickers, Hotchkiss and a few others – were actively involved in supplying the weapons. Though stories were circulated that the Germans had 50,000, the reality was that there were only about 2,500 in front-line service in July 1914. In addition, with national pride at stake, many armies had been hell-bent on developing designs of their own. Consequently, the French and the Italians, in particular, produced guns of questionable utility.

When the fighting dragged on into 1915 with no end in sight, the major armies learned some unwelcome lessons: the machine-gun was capable of prodigious slaughter, and even the most gallant cavalry charge could be suicidal. A notion had been put about (usually by

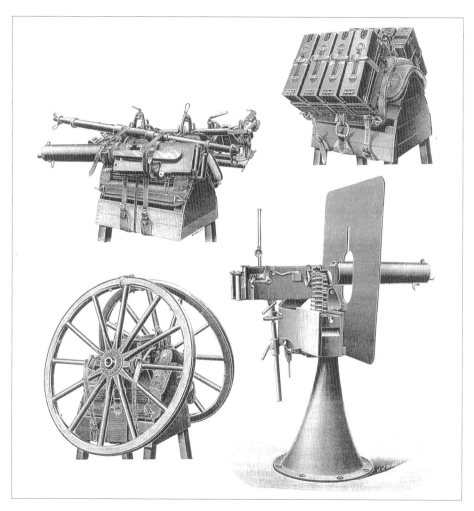

cavalrymen) that well-trained cavalry could simply ride-down machine-gunners at will, but combat showed this to be a dangerous myth. Yet generals were still sending men into withering machine-gun fire, and some units were reduced to a shambles by 'indirect fire' before even reaching the front line!

Vickers Guns, like comparable water-cooled Maxims and Brownings, were capable of amazing feats of endurance. Their potential became clear almost as soon as the First World War had begun: during the Battle of Loos (1915), for example, German Maxims reduced a twelve-battalion British assault from its initial strength of about 10,000 men to less than 2,000 in an hour. According to Lieutenant-Colonel Hutchinson, in his book Machine Guns, ten guns of his unit fired:

> ... During the attack of 24th August, 250 rounds short of one million ... Four two-gallon petrol tins of water, the company's water bottles, and all the urine tins from the neighbourhood were emptied into the guns for cooling purposes, an illustration of the amount of water consumed; while a party was employed throughout the action

Belgian soldiers crew a Maxim in a photograph taken c. 1910. Guns of this type served throughout the world.

A pre-1914 commercial-pattern Vickers Gun, mounted on a 1912-patent tripod secured to the ammunition cart.

carrying ammunition. Strict discipline as to barrel-changing was maintained. The company artificer, assisted by one private, maintained a belt filling machine in action without cessation for twelve hours. A prize of five francs to each of the members of the gun-team firing the greatest number of rounds was secured by the gun-teams of

Sergeant P. Dean, D.C.M., with a record of just over 120,000 rounds.

The utility of machine-guns was such that even captured weapons were pressed into front-line service. The British approved issue of the Maxim 'G', the German MG. 08, and the Germans

impressed large numbers of ex-Russian Maxims, converting many to fire the 8 x 57 rimless round. Surviving pre-1908 German ground guns (often taken from the navy) were issued for training purposes, freeing MG. 08 for front-line service; captured Vickers and Lewis Guns were turned against their former owners; and ex-Austrian Schwarzlose machine-guns were also used in small numbers by German units on the Austro-Italian front.

Once the value of machine-guns had been established and when the fighting had reached stalemate, particularly on the Western Front, thoughts turned to providing a weapon that could accompany raiding parties. The principal requirement for a gun of this type was light weight, though the metallurgical knowledge and production techniques of the day struggled to reach this particular goal.

Credit is usually given to Colonel Isaac Lewis of the US Army, an artilleryman who devised – 'developed' may be a better word – a successful gas-operated light machine-gun shortly before the First World War began. Lewis had a long and acrimonious battle with the US Army Chief of Ordnance, General Crozier, and progress with the gun was delayed until a manufacturing licence was concluded in Belgium. The ultimate success of the Lewis was due to the British Army, which ordered huge quantities from BSA in 1915.

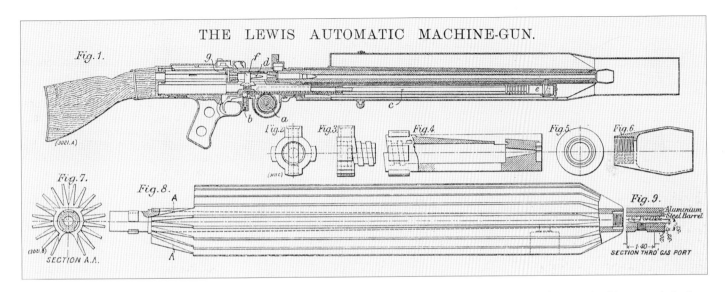

THE LEWIS AUTOMATIC MACHINE-GUN.

An early Lewis Gun, from Engineering, *8 November 1912. Changes had been made to the trigger and other parts of the action by 1914. Note that this gun lacks sights.*

However, credit for Lewis is based largely on an Anglo-American viewpoint. The first successful light machine-gun was unquestionably the Danish Madsen, introduced as early as 1902 in what was substantially its perfected form. Madsens had sold in quantity prior to 1914, and were used by the Allied and Central Powers forces alike during the First World War. The Germans acquired batches to equip Gebirgsjäger (mountain troops), and the Russians required sufficient to encourage Dansk Rekylriffel Syndikat to begin constructing a machine-gun factory in Kovrov. This did not become operational

until after the 1917 revolution, making Maxims, but showed that the demand for light machine-guns had been predicted in Europe prior to the First World War.

Only the Germans, who had made such good use of the heavy water-cooled Maxim, failed to introduce a true light machine-gun during the First World War. The MG. 08/15, a cumbersome water-cooled 'portable' variant of the standard MG. 08, was nothing other than a mistaken expedient. The problem was tactical: the

German goals were almost always centred on the desire to sustain fire instead of focusing on portability. Ironically, the air-cooled Bergmann aircraft guns pressed into ground roles at the end of the war proved to be much handier.

Another major problem, particularly in the German designs, was a preference for belt feed. This was also based on the desire to sustain fire, but made the 'light' guns heavy and difficult to carry. They became difficult for one man to operate,

A German gun-crew man what appears to be a captured 1910-pattern Russian Maxim machine-gun.

bolt designs, though the mechanism, a clever adaptation of the pivoting Peabody breech-block, was sturdy and reliable. The Lewis offered the advantages of a rotating bolt and a large-capacity horizontal pan magazine above the breech, but was complicated and prone to jamming. The French Chauchat (CSRG), a remarkable precursor of the cheap, easily made guns developed after 1918, was let down by poor metallurgy and inattention to detail. And the Browning Automatic Rifle, initially extremely successful in the hands of soldiers who could shoulder its excessive weight, was rarely used as a true light machine-gun.

The First World War was also the first conflict in which the machine-gun was used in the air and in armoured vehicles, each environment requiring the development of special features. The first vehicle guns – the British Hotchkiss, for example – were generally standard infantry guns with special sights, stocks and cartridge-case catchers. Aerial use, however, demanded much more thought. Many of the earliest warplanes were 'pushers', with the propeller mounted behind the pilot, and minor adaptations of ground guns could be fitted to slide or pillar mounts. But these aeroplanes were inefficient aerodynamically, and were soon abandoned in favour of 'tractor' designs, with the propeller at the nose.

and the value of portability was lost. The Madsen had a box magazine on top of the receiver, feeding downwards under a combination of spring and gravity, and had proved capable of handling a variety of rimmed and rimless cartridges. Its biggest problem was the lack of the primary extraction given by most rotating-

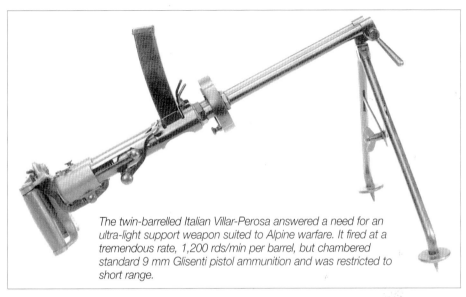

The twin-barrelled Italian Villar-Perosa answered a need for an ultra-light support weapon suited to Alpine warfare. It fired at a tremendous rate, 1,200 rds/min per barrel, but chambered standard 9 mm Glisenti pistol ammunition and was restricted to short range.

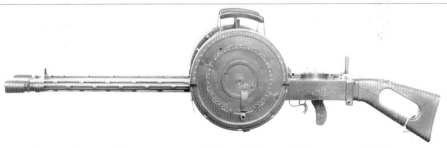

The German Gast machine-gun, patented in 1915–16, sought to provide sufficient fire-volume in the air, using two barrels and a cross-connected breech mechanism. The cumbersome drum magazines were a particular weakness of the design.

Guns were then mounted obliquely, which took great skill to employ effectively, or on rails that ran forward above the upper wing high enough to clear the propeller arc. It was soon realised that the most effective guns were fixed as near as possible to the longitudinal axis of the warplane, though single, centrally mounted engines presented problems. The most obvious place for the guns was ahead of the pilot, directly above the engine cowling where they were virtually in line with his eyes. This simplified aiming – the guns pointed the same way as the aeroplane flew – but the propeller would be directly in the bullet path. Some enterprising aviators fitted steel deflector plates to the propeller, trusting to fate and the comparatively low chance of a strike, but damage to propellers (and probably not a few fatal accidents) made a better solution obligatory.

The answer was found in the guise of synchronising gear, which ensured that the gun fired only when the bullet's path would be clear of the propeller blades. Many types of synchroniser were fitted, some proving more effective than others, and the pattern was set for many years. Used in conjunction with perfected ring-type mounts for observers' guns, synchronising gear was the perfect accessory for an airborne machine-gun.

Experience soon showed that the demands of aerial combat were very different from those of infantry support, and

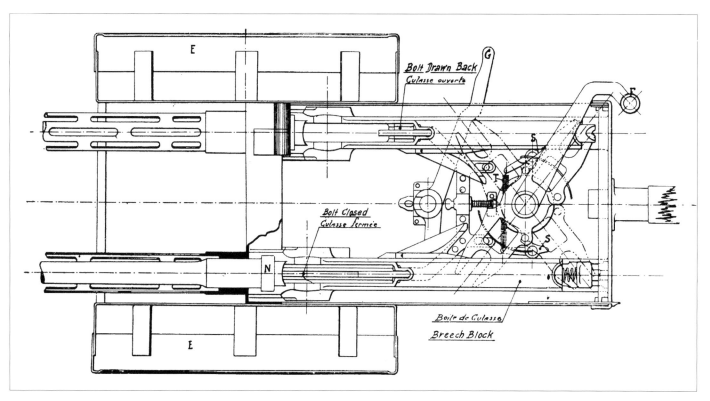

Labels in figure:
E

Bolt Drawn Back
Culasse ouverte
G
F
S
T
S

Bolt Closed
Culasse fermée

N

Boîte de Culasse
Breech Block

E

A French drawing of the breech mechanism of the Gast.

that 'little and often' was needed instead of protracted firing. In addition, guns used in the air were subject to stresses and strains induced by violent manoeuvring. Most countries attempted to convert their standard infantry machine-guns for aerial use, but often with unexpected results. The most successful adaptations were the Maxim group, which included the British Vickers and the German Parabellum. These had a robust feed system that relied more on mechanical operations than actuating springs; the German Bergmann, conversely, which was efficient enough in ground service, was soon withdrawn from air combat once it was realised that the spring-controlled feed system could not cope with rapid left-hand turns. The French, without an efficient land-service machine-gun other than the obsolescent Hotchkiss, used Vickers and Lewis Guns before adopting the lightweight Darne at the very end of hostilities. This and the cumbersome twin-barrelled German Gast were among the few wholly new designs to be introduced during the War.

When the fighting ceased, time could be taken to analyse the lessons that could be learned from combat in conditions ranging from the deadlocked trenchscape of the Western Front to the snowy subzero of the Eastern Front in winter and the arid sand of Mesopotamia. Though production of the Maxim ceased in Germany, huge numbers remained in circulation. Many were destroyed under the supervision of the Allied disarmament commission, though enough remained to equip not only the German police but also the armies of emergent nations such as Estonia, Latvia, Lithuania and Poland. Large numbers of Austro-Hungarian Schwarzlose machine-guns served Austria, Czechoslovakia and Hungary. The Russians retained the Maxim and the British clung to the Vickers Gun, which had proved themselves to be exceptionally reliable, and the US Army standardised the M1917 Browning – a wartime introduction that, once initial

teething troubles had been overcome, proved itself to be among the best of all infantry-support weapons. The Browning also proved itself to be an outstandingly successful air-cooled aircraft weapon.

Successful though many of the water-cooled heavy support weapons were, however, the situation with the light machine-guns was less encouraging. The Lewis was too complicated and too prone to jamming, and the French Chauchat ('CSRG') was too badly made to be reliable. The 'light' Hotchkiss was far too heavy, and the German MG. 08/15 was an unhappy hybrid. Experience had shown that recoil operation, ideal if the components could be robust (which suggested weight), was not suited to lightweight guns; the jarring as barrels and barrel-carriers moved backwards could be absorbed by a heavyweight gun but not on one that weighed less than 10 kg (22 lb). Only the first shot from the long-recoil Chauchat could be placed accurately, and the Fedorov automatic rifle (AVF) was exceptionally difficult to control when firing automatically… even though it had been deliberately chambered for a low-power cartridge.

The conflict between weight and power has never been satisfactorily solved in light machine-gun design: even modern guns such as the HK21 and the Minimi, which can feed from belts or box magazines, make sacrifices – the former in the difficulty of controlling automatic fire with the 7.62 mm

NATO round and the latter in the acceptance of a 5.56 mm cartridge that cannot be used satisfactorily in a fire-support role.

Though the Germans, in particular, had sought a 'universal' machine-gun, the so-called Einheitsmaschinengewehr, nothing of note had been achieved during the war. The Italians had introduced a small twin-barrelled 'machine-gun' to give mountain troops additional firepower, but this had been chambered for 9 mm handgun ammunition and proved to be a developmental dead-end. The embryonic submachine-guns such as the Bergmann also chambered pistol cartridges.

Experimentation undertaken between the wars, therefore, concentrated on developing efficient light machine-guns, providing aircraft guns with unusually high rates of fire, and developing large-calibre machine-guns (inspired by the anti-balloon guns of 1914–18) into battle-worthy weapons. A variety of light guns appeared during the 1920s, characterised by gas operation and, as often as not, breech-locking systems based on tilting blocks. This promised a simple and robust mechanism that did not need cam-tracks to be cut with great precision or parts that required too much machining. Only the Madsen remained to champion the virtues of recoil operation, comprehensively out-shooting its rivals in more than one trial held in the 1930s.

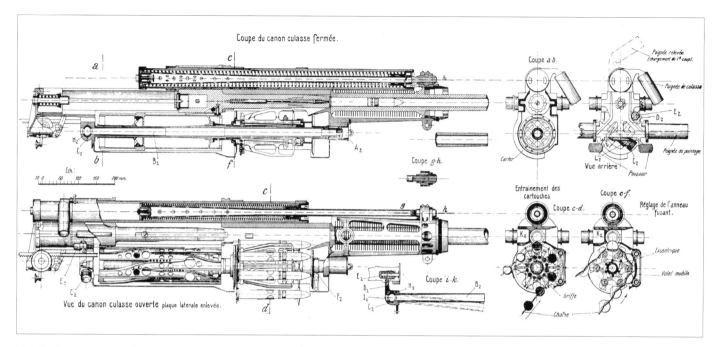

Coupe du canon culasse fermée.

This Szakatz cannon typifies the exceptional complexity of many machine-gun designs produced between the wars.

Among the first of the new gas-operated guns was the Berthier, subsequently exploited by Vickers but with origins pre-dating the First World War; cam fingers on the piston-rod extension acted on lugs on the breech-block to raise the tail of the block into the roof of the receiver. A specially hardened steel bar in the receiver, running transversely, minimised wear. The Czechoslovakian Praga and its derivatives (including the Bren Gun) were similar, but simpler and sturdier; the French Darne had a unique locking-piece inserted in the back of the breech-block, where it could be moved in and out of engagement with the receiver-roof by means of carefully designed cam surfaces; the 1922-type Hotchkiss retained a version of the familiar flap lock with pinned links; and the French Mle. 24/29 ('Châtellerault') relied on swinging links to control the movement of the breech-block.

If these guns were all successful, albeit in varying degrees, the same could not always be said of rival designs. The Italians went through a series of delayed blowbacks that required external lubrication to function properly, and even the locked-breech Breda, the best of the pre-1939 designs, could not escape the need for lubricated ammunition. The Italian magazines were also a peculiar bunch, ranging from hinged integral boxes to a tray system that took the cartridge out, fired it, and then replaced the spent case as the tray emerged from the opposite side of the breech. Some of the Japanese guns, based for the most part on the pre-1914 Hotchkiss, were no less quirky; the 11th Year Type and its tank-gun derivative, the Type 91, had a hopper magazine on the left side of the receiver, and the similar Type 96 (which had a box magazine) could even mount a bayonet.

The German designers became obsessed with the universal machine-gun.

The MG. 13 entered service in 1928, but was little more than a lightened air-cooled version of the pre-1918 Dreyse. The strut-type lock, inspired by a Mannlicher pistol design of the 1890s, was only marginally strong enough for its task, and the guns were relegated to secondary service as soon as better weapons became available.

The ultimate result was the MG. 34, derived from a design credited to Louis Stange of Rheinmetall. Initially made in Switzerland by Waffenfabrik Solothurn, guns of this type relied on a rotating locking collar inspired by the Hotchkiss Fermeture. They were used by the armies of Austria and Hungary from 1930 onward. The German derivative was a sophisticated product, issued with a bewildering multiplicity of mounts and

accessories. It had a double-trigger system to give single shots or automatic fire, and fed from a belt even when being used as a light machine-gun. A 75-round belt-drum was issued to enhance portability. Yet even the MG. 34 fell far short of operational requirements. It was too heavy and cumbersome to be an effective light machine-gun, and mounting it on a tripod camouflaged the lack of a heavy-support weapon comparable with the US Army .50 Browning or the Russian 12.7 mm DShK. The MG. 34 was also much too difficult, time-consuming and expensive to make, and proved to jam in hot and dusty or subzero conditions. But it was still being made in quantity in 1945 alongside its supposed replacement, the MG. 42.

When the Second World War began, light automatic weapons were often in short supply. The 'Charlton Rifle' was an ingenious conversion of a Lee-Enfield magazine rifle, developed in New Zealand and made in Australia. It worked much more efficiently than its crude appearance suggested.

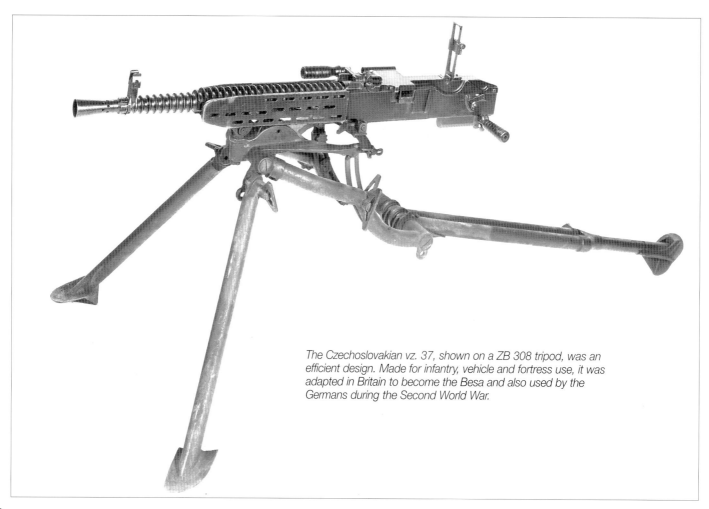

The Czechoslovakian vz. 37, shown on a ZB 308 tripod, was an efficient design. Made for infantry, vehicle and fortress use, it was adapted in Britain to become the Besa and also used by the Germans during the Second World War.

Elsewhere, the British adopted the Bren Gun – perhaps the best of all light machine-guns – and the US Army tinkered with the light machine-gun derivatives of the Browning Automatic Rifle, which, owing to their fixed barrels and small magazines, were unsuitable for even the light support role. Many specialised tank, vehicle and aircraft guns were developed, among the best known being the Brownings that served the USA, Britain and elsewhere during the Second World War.

Comparatively low rates of fire hindered the performance of many aircraft guns that had been derived from infantry patterns. This problem grew as aircraft speeds rose, and the 'window of opportunity' for an effective hit was progressively reduced.

Providing sufficient volume of fire was solved in several ways. Some designers favoured multi-gun installations, the British using as many as twelve 0.303-calibre Brownings in the Hurricane, and others developed multi-barrel guns. Some of the responses were much too complicated, particularly those where complexity was mistakenly seen as technological progress, but a few surprisingly fast-firing single-barrelled guns were made in quantity. Probably the most successful was the Soviet ShKAS, a rifle-calibre gun capable of attaining a fire-rate of 1,800–2,000 rds/min. The 'Ultra-ShKAS' and SN (Savin-Norov) machine-guns were both adopted officially by the USSR, though a pressing need for striking power at the expense of fire-rate prevented series production of either design. However, allowing the barrel to move forward as the breech ran back gave fire-rates as high as 3,000 rds/min in individual guns. Attempts were also made to cross-connect two individual ShKAS guns to produce a single unit with an exceptional rate of fire.

At the last moment, the Soviet designers saw sense. The 7.62 mm Ultra-ShKAS and SN were superseded by the 12.7 mm ShVAK and BS guns, each of which laid the basis for 20 mm adaptations created simply by changing the barrels. It is interesting that the Soviet authorities stripped all the Brownings out of the aircraft provided under wartime aid programmes, replacing them with the reliable and often more powerful indigenous weapons.

When the Second World War began, few armies, perhaps excepting the Germans, possessed sufficient machine-guns to support lengthy large-scale campaigns. The shortages reflected the situation in 1914. In Britain, production of Vickers Guns was accelerated in 1939–40, but the weapon was complicated and notoriously difficult to make. Total output during the Second World War, at least according to the Contract Books, amounted to merely 17,400 0.303 Mk I Land Service guns (new and refurbished), plus 2,700 Mks VI and VII vehicle guns. There were also 1,117 0.50-calibre Vickers Guns on hand on 1 January 1940. The production of Vickers gun contrasts with the output of Bren Guns, which exceeded 400,000.

In desperation, the British ordered 1,000 7.9 mm Vickers Guns from Belgium, and stores were ransacked for obsolescent guns. These included about 11,000 Hotchkiss light machine-guns refurbished in 1940–1 by Enfield, BSA Guns Ltd, Boss & Co., Westley Richards and John Rigby & Co. The Lend-Lease scheme then contributed more than 12,000 0.30 M1915 (ground) and .30 M1918 (air) Vickers Guns in 1940–1, as well as 15,600 M1917 Marlin aircraft guns and 2,600 M1918 Marlin tank guns, and large quantities of Lewis Guns were also acquired. Somehow, the British 'muddled through' to 1945.

Even the Soviet forces obtained a considerable amount of foreign matériel from various sources. Among the machine-guns were the Czechoslovakian ZB vz. 26; German MG. 08, MG. 08/15, MG. 13, MG. 34 and MG. 42; British Vickers and Vickers-Berthier; American Colt M1914 and Browning M1917.

Progress in the Soviet Union was hindered by the German invasion in June

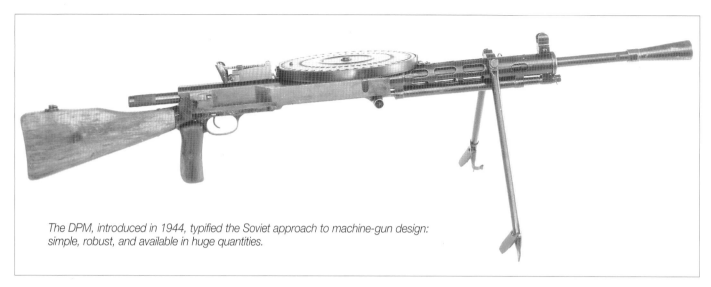

The DPM, introduced in 1944, typified the Soviet approach to machine-gun design: simple, robust, and available in huge quantities.

1941, which severely disrupted the arms industry and forced the evacuation not only of personnel but also of entire factories. And there was also a political dimension in the USSR that was rare elsewhere. For example, Stalin favoured the much-decorated Degtyarev and could not understand why the army wished to adopt the GVG (the prototype SG-43) to replace the Maxim. Only when Vasiliy Degtyarev bravely stated that the GVG was a better design than his own gun, an improved version of the unsuccessful DS, did Stalin relent.

The simplicity of the indigenous Soviet designs contrasted with the sophistication of the German equipment. The MG. 34 and MG. 42 were no match for the Degtyarev, Maxim and Goryunov machine-guns they faced. The Soviet weapons were undoubtedly crude by comparison, lacking the range of sophisticated sights and mounts, and were prone to stoppages caused by bad quality control and variations in the ammunition. Yet they worked in conditions where the Germans guns did not, and the 12.7 mm DShK gave the Red Army the effective infantry-support weapon that the Wehrmacht lacked.

The British and the Americans retained the Vickers and the Browning infantry guns for the duration of the war, though the water-cooling system of the M1917A1 Browning had given way to air-cooling on the M1919A4 and M1919A6. The Bren Gun remained in production throughout hostilities, in Canada as well as Britain, though the Vickers-Berthier was retained in the Indian Army until 1943. Efforts were also made to develop ultra-simple designs in 1940–1, immediately after the loss of Brens at Dunkirk and the realisation that a bombing raid on Enfield, then the sole source of Bren Guns in Britain, would disrupt supplies. The best of the emergency guns, the Besal or Faulkner, was adopted in 1943; by that time, however, the crisis had passed and the new weapon was never made in quantity. Similarly, the promising recoil-operated Johnson light machine-gun, which weighed merely 12.8 lb in its perfected 1944 form, never enticed the US Army strongly enough to be used for anything other than special purposes.

Impressments of captured weapons, no problem when armies were winning, proved to be a handicap when the great retreats began. The guns that chambered non-standard ammunition were particularly vulnerable to the hasty evacuation of territory and the loss of stores. But a similar problem could arise from poor control over the design and development of small arms in peacetime. By the end of the Second World War, the Japanese ground forces held such an incredible variety of regulation machine-guns that no fewer than eight basic cartridges were needed: two 6.5 mm, three 7.7 mm, one 7.9 mm, one 12.7 mm and one 13.2 mm. The Germans encountered similar logistical complications with the broad range of guns that had been taken in 1938-43.

When the war ended, the Western Allies were equipped with efficient machine-guns, even though the Vickers and the Browning had pre-1918 origins. The Bren Gun had proved its value, but thoughts were turning instead to the concept of a universal machine-gun – even though the German MG. 34 and MG. 42 had each been failures in their own way: the former largely because it was too well made, and the latter because its excessive rate of fire was little more than a waste of ammunition. The Soviet Army had the DPM, a pan-fed Degtyarev that was efficient but limited; the SG or Goryunov, which had been a great success once manufacturing problems had been overcome; and the large-calibre DShK.

Some of these machine-guns were made in huge numbers, though it is difficult to provide accurate totals. The USA is said to have made 2.6 million guns between the attack on Pearl Harbor (7 December 1941) and the end of the campaigns in the Far East (August 1945); German output in 1939–45 totalled 1.2 million; and Soviet claims suggest that more than 1.5 million machine-guns of all types and calibres were made during the Great Patriotic War (22 June 1941–8 May 1945). British production in 1939–44 amounted to less than a million machine-guns, though output must be considered in relation to other small arms. The USA and the USSR made roughly comparable quantities of rifles – more than 12 million apiece – and the German output exceeded 10 million. British rifle production amounted merely to 2.5 million, but then Britain produced more submachine-guns than any other nation excepting the USSR.

One of the ironies of the post-war analysis was the emphasis given (some would argue, unfairly) to German developments, forgetting the adage that efficiency may decline as the number of parts grows. The results have been to dwell on the MG. 42 (now known as the 'MG. 3'), which remains impossible to control when fired from a bipod, and the introduction of intermediate cartridges that are incapable of fulfilling the long-range support role previously undertaken by rifle-calibre guns such as Maxims, Vickers and Brownings.

The problems of providing adequate light machine-guns have supposedly been eased by the introduction of heavy-barrelled rifles with selective-fire capabilities, but combat has often shown this strategy to be flawed.

Consequently, guns such as the Bren, adapted to fire the 7.62 mm NATO cartridge, survived in front-line service until recent years. There are those who still consider the 5.56 mm Minimi to be a poor replacement … and there is still no adequate replacement for the legendary .50-calibre Browning in western armies!

Škoda M1893 Austria-Hungary

The 1902-type Škoda retained the hopper magazine.

This was one of the stranger designs to see military service. The Austro-Hungarian authorities had purchased 160 Maxims in 1889, chambered for the 8 x 52 cartridge; these were successful enough to remain in service for many years, suitably upgraded in 1891 and 1904, and a few survivors were still being held in reserve in 1914. However, the authorities had often shown that

they were reluctant to pay licensing fees if an indigenous design could be found. This explained the adoption of the Werndl rifle, and also the favours given to the Škoda machine-gun.

The Škoda was designed in the 1880s by Archduke Karl Salvator and Ritter von Dormus, which was sufficient in itself to guarantee that any failings would be underplayed. The two-part breech-block assembly was a form of delayed blowback. When the gun was fired, pressure acting through the base of the cartridge case tried to force the front block or 'breech piece' backward, against the pressure of a powerful return spring and the inertia required to rotate the supporting piece from its rest position. This was enough the delay the opening stroke long enough for chamber pressure to drop to safe levels. The spent case was ejected, and the spring then returned the parts, pivoting the breech-block components into position.

The original Škoda had a water jacket, a hopper-type magazine on the left side of the breech, and an oil reservoir alongside the magazine case. An oscillating oiler lubricated each cartridge before it entered the breech. The strangest feature, however, was a

pendulum lever beneath the return-spring chamber that could be adjusted to vary the rate of fire.

Adopted in October 1893 to supersede the Maxim (which was probably only ever seen as a stop-gap), the Škoda was made only in small numbers. It cannot be mistaken for any other machine-gun, owing to its idiosyncratic design, but seems to have worked reliably in favourable conditions. Like most delayed blowbacks, however, extraction was probably poor in cold or dusty environments, and it is suspected that the lubricator was only a partial answer to the problem. The cooling system also depended on a separate manually operated force pump. The guns are very well made, but typical of the ineffectual first-generation designs that sought to circumvent Maxim's patents.

The M1893 was superseded by the M1902, which retained the same basic design, and then by an unsuccessful M1903 'cavalry' pattern. The rejection of the latter in favour of the Schwarzlose forced Škoda's technicians to make radical changes to the basic weapon.

Model 1909. A simplification of the basic design, this fed from a fabric belt instead of the hopper, the rate-regulator

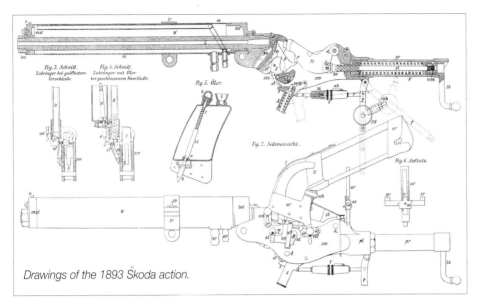

Fig.3. Schnitt. Zubringer bei geöffnetem Verschlusse.

Fig.4. Schnitt. Zubringer mit Öler bei geschlossenem Verschlusse.

Fig.5. Öler.

Fig.2. Seitenansicht.

Fig.6. Aufsatz.

Drawings of the 1893 Škoda action.

Designation: Maschinengewehr Škoda, Modell 1893
Made by Actiengesellschaft Škoda, Pilsen

Specification: Standard M1909
Data taken from John Walter, Central Powers' Small Arms of World War One (1999)
Calibre: 8 mm (0.315 in)
Chambering: 8 x 50 mm, rimmed
Operation: automatic; delayed blowback
Locking system: delay is provided by the shaping of the breech-block assembly
Length: 1,045 mm (41.2 in)
Weight: of gun 15.5 kg (34.2 lb)
Barrel: 570 mm (22.4 in), four grooves, right-hand twist
Mount: tripod
Feed system: fabric belt, 100 or 250 rounds
Muzzle velocity: 575 m/sec (1,885 ft/sec) with standard ball ammunition
Cyclic rate: 420 rds/min (variable)

was abandoned, the oil tank was moved to the top of the receiver, and the diameter of the water jacket was increased to allow the pump to be discarded. The trigger protruded from the rear underside of the receiver. The tripod was improved and a compact German-type optical sight could be fitted to a bracket on the rear left side of the breech. Only a handful of guns (perhaps 30) were used by the Austro-Hungarian forces, survivors of a small batch that had been sold to China but never delivered.

The Škoda M1909.

Designed by a German, Andreas Schwarzlose, this was patented in its original form in 1902. The inventor agreed terms with Österreichische Waffenfabriks-Gesellschaft and guns were sent for trials with the Austro-Hungarian army. They proved to be sturdy and durable, but were susceptible to jamming and case-head separations. The problem was cured simply by shortening the barrel, and the Schwarzlose was adopted officially in 1907. The earliest guns could be identified by their 'humped' appearance, with a noticeable gap between the front of the receiver and the barrel jacket. A mechanical oil-pump was

fitted to lubricate the cartridges as they entered the chamber, and folding grips were provided at the rear of the spring chamber that projected from the receiver.

Schwarzlose machine-guns were successful commercially, 6.5 mm-calibre versions being made under licence in Sweden and the Netherlands. The Steyr factory supplied 8 x 50R guns to Bulgaria, accompanying consignments of Mannlicher rifles, and small quantities were sent to Greece during the Balkan War of 1912–13. These chambered the 6.5 x 54 rimless cartridge.

M1907/12. Experience revealed teething problems with the M1907, and a modified pattern was substituted in 1912. This had a straight-topped receiver, lacking the characteristic gap, and the oil pump was replaced by a lubricating pad. Minor changes were also made to the trigger system. The M1907/12 remained in service throughout the First World War, proving efficient enough to escape all but the most minor alterations. However, night firing emphasised the excessive 'firing flash' from such a short barrel, and most ground guns were given long conical flash-hiders.

Schwarzlose machine-guns were made in large numbers, production in the Österreichische Waffenfabriks-Gesellschaft factory in Steyr amounting to at least 50,000 during the war. Many survivors were given to Yugoslavia in the early 1920s, and others, often converted for the 7.9 x 57 mm rimless round, were used in Czechoslovakia (q.v.). Some of the guns retained by the Austrian and Hungarian armies were converted in the 1930s for the 8 x 56 mm round ('M30' in Austria, '31.M' in Hungary), pending the introduction of better weapons.

M1907/16. The Schwarzlose was also the standard Austro-Hungarian aircraft gun, altered so that the barrel protruded from the

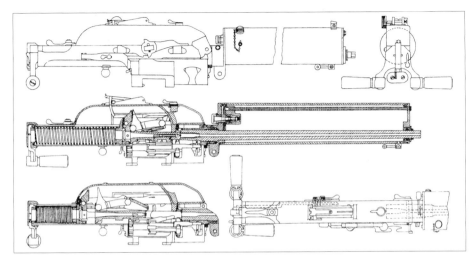

Drawings of the M1907 Schwarzlose action.

receiver and a front sight could be mounted on an extension bar. The earliest of these air-cooled guns were made in the Vienna Fliegerarsenal by converting ground guns, and often had a small part of the original water jacket near the breech; later ones were purpose-built. The return springs were more robust than normal, raising the cyclic rate to about 500 rds/min. The M1907/16A was a high-speed version, with extra-strong springs and a muzzle booster designed to increase the cyclic rate to 800 rds/min. The work was undertaken by the Löhner factory in Vienna in 1918, but taxed the delayed blowback system to its limits.

M1912/16. This was a 'light machine-gun' derivative of the M1907/12, mounted on a small tripod and with a shoulder pad extending back from the spring housing. The Austro-Hungarians had purchased more than 600 6.5 mm Danish Madsens in 1915, but the conversion to chamber the German 8 x 57 cartridge had taken so long that something else was needed – though the converted Schwarzlose, which retained the water jacket, was scarcely ideal for the role even when issued with special 100-round ammunition belts.

A typical M1907/12 Schwarzlose machine-gun. This gun lacks a flash-hider.

Designation: Maschinengewehr Schwarzlose Modell 1907
Made by Österreichische Waffenfabriks-Gesellschaft, Steyr ('OEWG')

Specification: Standard M1907/12
Data taken from John Walter, Central Powers' Small Arms of World War One (1999)
Calibre: 8 mm (0.315 in)
Chambering: 8 x 50, rimmed
Operation: automatic; delayed blowback
Locking system: none; the toggle-joint interfaces provided the necessary delay
Length: 1,070 mm (42.1 in) without flash-hider
Weight: 19.3 kg (42.6 lb) without mount
Barrel: 528 mm (20.8 in), four grooves, right-hand twist
Mount: tripod
Feed system: fabric belt, 100 or 250 rounds
Muzzle velocity: 575 m/sec (1,885 ft/sec) with standard ball ammunition
Cyclic rate: 400 rds/min

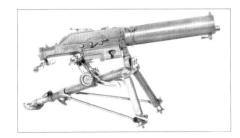

Steyr-Solothurn M1930   Austria

The Austrian M30 and Hungarian 31.M guns were identical mechanically, though the latter had an auxiliary handgrip in front of the trigger.

The German Rheinmetall company, known prior to 1927 as 'Rheinische Metallwaaren- & Maschinenfabrik', had been a leading producer of small arms and munitions during the First World War – so prominent that the Allies forbade the company to make anything but artillery after 1919.

Keen to evade these restraints, Rheinmetall had participated in the formation of Hollandsche Artillerie-Industrie en Handelsmaatschappij ('HAIHA') in the Netherlands in the early 1920s and, when this enterprise failed to prosper, had created Wffenfabrik Solothurn AG (effectively a Swiss subsidiary) before reaching an arrangement with Steyr-Daimler-Puch.

The principal novelty in the machine-gun design, which was attributed to Louis Stange, Rheinmetall's designer, lay in the method of locking. As the barrel, barrel extension and bolt recoiled, a rotating collar on the barrel extension was cammed out of engagement with an interrupted screw on the bolt. When the barrel and barrel extension stopped, the bolt reciprocated alone. It was then returned by the recoil spring and stripped another cartridge into the breech.

The Rh. 29 light machine-gun prototype soon became the Solothurn S2-200. Offered for sale in a variety of chamberings, this gun initially generated very little interest, though a few were sold to El Salvador in 1932 and impressive tests were undertaken in Austria and Hungary. Production of the Austrian 'Modell 30' began in the Steyr-Daimler-Puch factory, and the Hungarian '31.M' in the Fegyvergyar ('FÉG') plant in Budapest.

Both of these guns chambered the rimmed 8 x 56 mm cartridge, but the later Hungarian 43.M shared the German 7.9 x 57 mm rimless cartridge and an MG. 13-pattern box magazine.

Designation: Maschinengewehr Modell 1930
Made by Steyr-Werke AG (Steyr-Daimler-Puch AG from 1934), Steyr

Specification: Standard Austrian infantry pattern
Data taken from Ian Hogg and John Weeks, Military Small Arms of the Twentieth Century, seventh edition, 2000
Calibre: 8 mm (0.315 in)
Chambering: 8 x 56, rimmed
Operation: selective fire; short recoil
Locking system: rotating bolt
Length: 1,174 mm (46.25 in)
Weight: 7.8 kg (17.3 lb)
Barrel: 596 mm (23.5 in), four grooves, right-hand twist
Mount: bipod
Feed system: detachable box magazine, 25 rounds
Muzzle velocity: 730 m/sec (2,395 ft/sec) with standard ball ammunition
Cyclic rate: 800 rds/min

Maxim Gun Britain

British soldiers clean their 0.303 Mk I Maxim Gun in camp, c. 1902. Note the size and clumsiness of the carriage.

After undertaking extensive trials, the War Office approved the 0.45-calibre Mark I Maxim Guns for issue to infantry battalions 'for instructional purposes' in 1890, but the programme was still incomplete when the South African or 'Boer' War began in 1899. The large-calibre guns had been supplemented in 1892 by the 'Gun, Maxim, 0.303-inch Mark I, Magazine Rifle Chamber' and many of the 0.45 examples were eventually converted to become '0.303 Converted, Mark I' guns. Most of them remained in second-line service throughout the First World War, though nominally replaced after 1912 by the Vickers Gun (see below).

The earliest British Maxims were accompanied by cumbersome wheeled carriages, beginning with the 'Carriage, Naval, Machine Gun, Mk I' (1887) and ending with the 'Carriage, Field, Machine Gun, Infantry, Maxim, Mk III' of 1900. Cavalry carriages were all large and very high, however, with the bore axis of the gun being at shoulder height. Mark III infantry carriages remaining in service after c. 1912 also carried a Mark IV tripod to enable the gun to be dismounted.

There were also four Maxim tripods, Marks I–IV, introduced in 1897–1906.

The original Mark I had fixed legs and a limited traverse; the Mark III was the first to have folding legs. There was also a 'Mounting, Cone, Maxim, Mark I' and three 'Parapet Carriages' (1888, 1895 and 1899). Parapet carriages were uncommon, the Mark III Maxim pattern being introduced specifically for service in Gibraltar.

Maxims had proved devastating during the Matabele Campaign and at the Battle of Omdurman (1898), where they have been credited with three-quarters of the casualties inflicted on the Dervishes. During the Boer War (1899–1902), unfortunately, they were used ineptly – machine-guns were still often seen as light artillery – and the cumbersome wheeled carriages were vulnerable to the enemy fire.

Maxim machine-guns are all recoil-operated. The barrel recoils far enough to break the toggle-lock, and is then brought to a halt. The toggle continues to break downward as the spent case is extracted from the chamber, a new round is pulled backward from the belt, and an empty case is positioned behind the ejection chute. When the toggle has come to the end of its travel, and is folded in the rear of the receiver, the return spring or 'fusee', mounted externally on the left side of the receiver and protected by a light sheet-steel cover, pulls the toggle

Lord Dundonald's Galloper Carriage (1898) was an early attempt to improve the mobility of the Maxim.

mechanism back. As it moves forward, the feed block has dropped until the cartridge taken from the belt is aligned with the chamber and the spent case is directly behind the previous spent case. The toggle continues to expand, thrusting the cartridge into the chamber and using the spent case to expel the original case from the gun. At the end

of the stroke the mechanism is relocked, and the feed block rises to its starting position. The gun can then be fired and the entire cycle begins again.

The Maxim was very efficient, though comparatively bulky. Production was originally slow; most guns were made for military trials and the orders, if they were agreed at all,

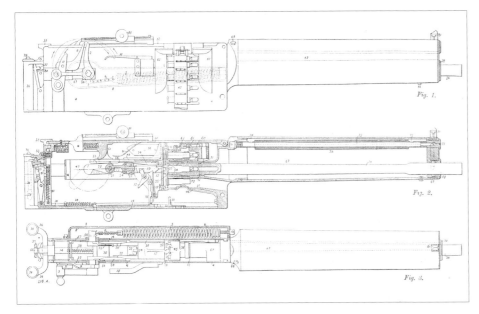

Sections of a Maxim Gun, from Engineering, *9 October 1891.*

were customarily for handfuls. The success of the Maxim in the hands of the Russians during the Russo-Japanese War was an important publicity coup, but had comparatively little effect. Excepting the German MG. 08 and the Russian/Soviet PM, described separately, very few Maxim-type guns were made in quantity and the design was superseded in Britain

by the Vickers Gun. However, the 0.303 in Maxim was not declared obsolete in British service until 1928.

Some of the Maxims used outside Britain and Germany are listed in Appendix 1. Longstaff and Atteridge, in The Book of the Machine Gun (1917), note the users as Britain, Germany, Russia, Switzerland, Spain, Italy, the Netherlands, Sweden, Turkey, Greece, Denmark, Portugal, Romania and the USA. Many war-surplus guns served newly emergent nations such

as Poland after the end of the First World War.

Designation: Gun, Machine, Maxim, 0.303-inch Mark I
Made by the Maxim Gun Co. Ltd (1884–8), the Maxim-Nordenfelt Guns & Ammunition Co. Ltd (1888–97) and Vickers, Sons & Maxim Ltd, Crayford, Kent

Specification: Standard pattern
Data taken from Ian Hogg and
    John Weeks, Military Small Arms of
    the Twentieth Century, seventh edition,
    2000
Calibre: 7.7 mm (0.303 in)
Chambering: 0.303 in (7 x 56R)
Operation: automatic; short recoil
Locking system: toggle joint, breaking
    downward
Length: 1,076 mm (42.4 in)
Weight: 27.2 kg (60.0 lb)
Barrel: 711 mm (28.0 in), four grooves,
    right-hand twist
Mount: tripod (see also text)
Feed system: fabric belt, 250 rounds
Muzzle velocity: 548 m/sec (1,800
    ft/sec) with standard Mk I ball
    ammunition
Cyclic rate: 400 rds/min

Vickers Gun

A typical 0.303 Mark I Vickers Gun.

Developed in the early twentieth century, the Vickers is simply a Maxim Gun with the locking mechanism inverted so that the toggle breaks upward. The patents were granted in 1908–10 in the names of Arthur Dawson ('superintendent of ordnance works') and George Buckham ('engineer'), but it is likely that the details were left to a team within the Vickers-Armstrongs factory.

The changes were made to lighten the Maxim action, without sacrificing strength, but the Vickers machine-gun was still comparatively cumbersome. The operation of the locking mechanism and feed system is very similar to the Maxim (q.v.), except

that the toggle is reversed. This allows the receiver to be considerably shallower, as a comparison between the Vickers drawings below and the Maxim drawings previously will show. Most guns had tangent or tangent-leaf back sights, often placed well forward above the feed block. Muzzle boosters were commonly fitted to increase the cyclic rate from 300 rds/min to 450 rds/min.

Mark I. Introduced in November 1912 and issued with the 'Mounting, Machine-gun, Tripod, Mark IV', dating from 1906, this replaced the older Maxim (q.v.). Purchases were meagre, however; the British authorities had acquired merely 108 Maxim and Vickers guns in 1904–14.

The Mk IV mount was eventually superseded by the essentially similar Mk IVB, with a smaller traverse ring, and

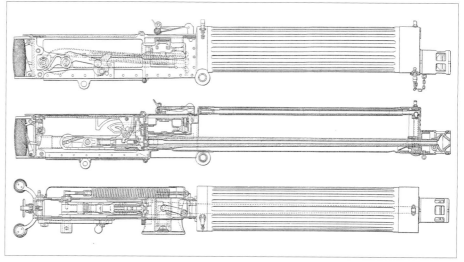

Sections of the Vickers Gun, from a Vickers, Sons & Maxim handbook dated 1910.

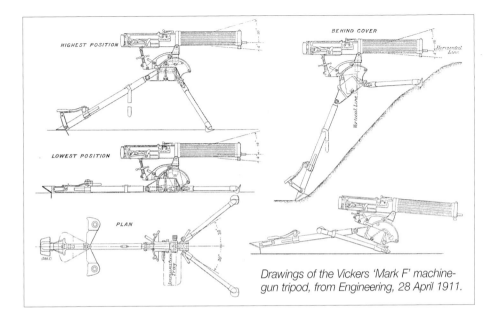

HIGHEST POSITION

BEHIND COVER

LOWEST POSITION

PLAN

Drawings of the Vickers 'Mark F' machine-gun tripod, from Engineering, 28 April 1911.

the high profile of the gun and gunner was only partially solved by the issue of the 'Mounting, Overbank, Machine-gun, Mark I'. This enabled the Vickers to be raised above the parapet of a dug-out, to fire on pre-determined paths, without the gunner exposing himself or his weapon unnecessarily.

That the Vickers Mk I was the only Land Service pattern ever to be introduced was a testimony to its reliability, excepting occasional jams caused by the rimmed ammunition. The

Vickers saw service in all theatres of war, in armoured vehicles and in aircraft, and was not declared obsolete until 1968.

The water jacket, fluted for additional rigidity, held about seven pints. Once the gun had been fired long enough for the water to reach boiling point (200–250 rds/min for three minutes), evaporation was approximately 12 pints for each additional 1,000 rounds once the water had begun to boil. Steam was then led off through a hose into a condenser can, from which water could subsequently be

poured back into the jacket. The inevitable reduction in coolant was made good from any available source, which could be a neighbouring stream, water bottles, urine or even wine.

Accuracy could be ruined by prolonging firing too long, as the heat generated was so great that the barrel could expand to a point where the bullets failed to engrave in the rifling. If shooting persisted beyond this point, the barrel could be ruined. Consequently, it was wise to replace the barrel at regular intervals. This was done by elevating the gun and pulling the barrel backward, inserting a large cork into the aperture in the front of the barrel jacket. The gun was then depressed and the barrel withdrawn backwards. A new barrel was simply slid into the gun forwards, relying on greased asbestos string wrapped to act as a seal, and knocking the cork out of the muzzle aperture. Water was allowed to drain from the bore and another 10,000 rounds could be fired before the next change was necessary.

Mark I* (February 1918). An Air Service gun, this had a large-diameter barrel jacket with cooling louvres and an open front end-cap. The steam tube was omitted.

Mark II (June 1917). This could be distinguished from the Mk I* by a smaller barrel casing and the omission of the fusee spring box from the left side of the receiver.

The 1912-patent Vickers 'Mark F' tripod in an over-bank role.

Mark II* (June 1927). Another of the Air Service guns, this was similar to the Mk II but had an extended cocking lever. 'A'-type guns fed from the left, and 'B'-type guns fed from the right.

Mark III ('A' and 'B' types). These guns had extended flash-hiders, which increased overall length to about 49 in.

Mark IV. Intended to be used in armoured vehicles, the Mk IV A (left-hand feed) and Mk IV B (right-hand feed) were introduced 'for the record' in 1930 but immediately declared obsolete. They had been converted from Mk I Vickers Guns, receiving new mounting plates, trunnion blocks and barrel casings.

Mark V (1933?). This was an Air Service gun, similar to the Mk III but with a top cover that hinged laterally. It was declared obsolete in 1944.

Marks VI A and VI B (August 1934). These were vehicle guns with strengthened dovetail mountings, alloy fusee spring covers and fluted barrel casings. They were otherwise identical with the Mk IV, weighed about 41½ lb, and were declared obsolete in August 1944.

Mark VI* ('A' and 'B' types). Conversions of Mk I Land Service guns for use in armoured vehicles, these were adapted to trunnion blocks with connections for the cooling system in the vehicles. The barrel casing was fluted and the guns weighed about 42½ -43 lb without water. The guns were declared obsolete in 1944.

Mark VII. A modified Mk VI, this had an improved mounting dovetail that was integral with the ejection-tube sleeve. The barrel casing was plain, and the guns weighed 47¾ lb. Guns of this type were obsolete in 1944.

Export patterns. The Vickers Gun, like the Maxim before it, was marketed commercially prior to 1914. These guns were offered in a variety of chamberings, and, excepting those supplied to colonial forces (which were accompanied by British regulation tripods) were usually mounted on Vickers' own tripods. The 1911-patent design, for example, allowed firing from the prone position or over a bank. Only a few guns were exported prior to 1914, though attempts were still being made to interest Brazil as late as 1935. Argentina (7.65 mm), Bolivia (7 mm) and Paraguay (7 mm) are known to have placed small orders prior to 1918. In addition, Colt made a few thousand 0.30 in M1915 guns for the US Army prior to the adoption of the Browning, and some of these were sold to Mexico in the early 1920s.

Designation: Gun, Machine, Vickers, ·303-inch Mark I
Made by Vickers Ltd, Crayford, Kent, and Erith (closed 1931), Kent

Specification: Standard Mk I infantry pattern
Data taken from Ian Hogg and
    John Weeks, Military Small Arms of the
    Twentieth Century, seventh edition,
    2000
Calibre: 7.7 mm (0.303 in)
Chambering: 0.303 in (7 x 56R)
Operation: automatic; short recoil
Locking system: toggle joint, breaking upward
Length: 1,155 mm (45.5 in)
Weight: 18.1 kg (40.0 lb)
Barrel: 723 mm (28.5 in), four grooves, right-hand twist
Mount: Mk IVB tripod, 22.7 kg (50.0 lb)
Feed system: fabric belt, 250 rounds
Muzzle velocity: 745 m/sec (2,450 ft/sec) with standard Mk VIIIZ ball ammunition
Cyclic rate: 450 rds/min

A Vickers 'Mark D' 0.50 machine-gun on a cone mount.

0.5 in patterns

Small quantities of a large-calibre Vickers Gun were also produced, similar to the rifle-calibre patterns but lacking the muzzle booster. The feed was altered to handle rimless cartridges.

Mark I (August 1933). This was a semi-experimental Land Service gun. The barrel had a distinctive conical flash-hider, and a delay pawl in the rear handle held the crank until the barrel had been returned to battery. The water-cooled gun could be fed from either side, with a few minor modifications, and would receive a tripod. Empty, it

weighed 52lb. Excepting the Mk. III, all 0.5 Vickers machine-guns were declared obsolete in August 1944.

Mark II (February 1932). This was a vehicle gun with an angled pistol grip. Like the Mk I, but unlike some of the later guns, it could fire single shots or fully automatically.

Mark III (1933?). A water-cooled Naval Service gun, this was converted from the Mk I. Removing the delay pawl and strengthening the buffer spring raised the cyclic rate from 450 to about 700 rds/min. Disintegrating-link belts were used.

Mark IV (November 1933). An improved vehicle gun, few of these were ever made. They could feed from either side of the breech. Compared with the Mk II, the Mk IV had a narrow dovetail plate and mounting

A Vickers Mk I 'in action' during the First World War. Note the small auxiliary tripod strapped beneath the water jacket.

base facilitating interchangeability with 0.303 vehicle guns. It weighed 58 lb empty.

Mark V (1935?). These vehicle guns were similar to the Mk IV, but had detachable ejection tubes and reinforced mounts.

Commercial patterns. Vickers sold machine-guns throughout the world, often in conjunction with aircraft and armoured vehicles. The 'Mark C' (1923) was similar mechanically to the British service machine-guns, but was lighter. The diameter of the barrel jacket was reduced, the receiver was shallower, and the back sight was often a patented Vickers design. Conical flash-hiders, cut diagonally to act as compensators, were also normally present. Mounts could be tripods, pillars or cones, and the barrels of aircraft guns were usually supported by plates extending forward from the receiver-sides.

The 'Mark D' (also known as the 'Model D') was introduced in the early 1930s to compete with guns such as the 13.2 x 99 Hotchkiss, which fired much more powerful cartridges than the Vickers 12.7 x 81 pattern. Also known by its project number, V/664, the new 12.7 mm round had a case measuring 119 mm. The actions were lengthened to accommodate the new round, though the guns remained mechanically identical with the Mark C. Mark D* guns offered improvements in the sights, and also had flash-hiders.

Lewis Gun Britain

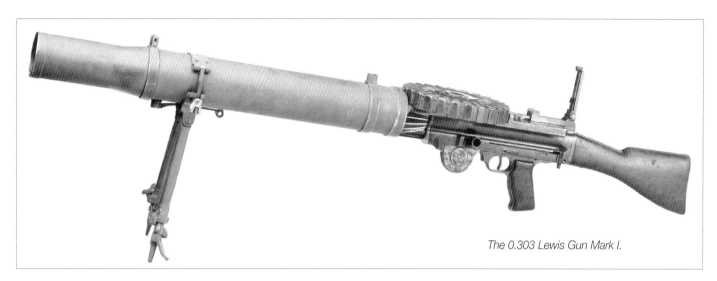

The 0.303 Lewis Gun Mark I.

Though they were ruthlessly efficient, Maxim and Vickers Guns were difficult and expensive to make. In addition, their weight and reliance on water-cooling confined them to static emplacements. Something else was needed to support infantrymen as they crossed No Man's Land. A solution was found in the pan-fed Lewis Gun, developed in the USA but licensed to BSA by way of Armes Automatiques Lewis of Liége in 1913. When the British government cast around for machine-guns late in 1914, therefore, BSA was ready. The Mark I Lewis Gun was approved on 15 October 1915, but series production had been underway for some time.

The Lewis was prone to jamming, owing to the complexity of its spring-feed magazine and problems feeding rimmed cartridges, but the men accepted this failing in return for its mobility. If a magazine jammed, it was simply discarded in favour of the next one.

Defective pans were repaired when (or if) their firers got back to British trenches.

The standard British Land Service Lewis was air-cooled, but incorporated a forced-draught system. The barrel was encased in a ribbed aluminium radiator inserted in a plain cylindrical jacket. The mouth of the jacket, which was partially open, projected in front of the muzzle. Expansion of propellant gases at the muzzle was supposed to draw air in from the rear of the radiator, along the

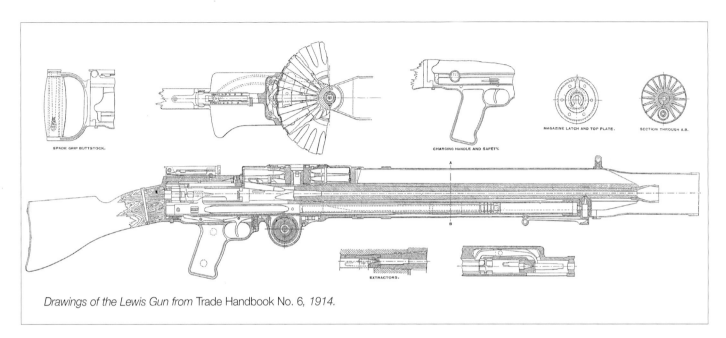

Drawings of the Lewis Gun from Trade Handbook No. 6, *1914.*

ribs and out of the muzzle opening. It is suspected that the Lewis would have been as efficient, and also several pounds lighter, without the cooling system.

BSA alone made more than 145,000 for the British, Belgians and Russians during the war, and the firepower of the infantry was soon increased. The Lewis Gun was the standard British light machine-gun until replaced by the Bren Gun in the 1930s. However, substantial quantities survived to serve the Home Guard and the Merchant Navy throughout the Second World War. The Mark I was declared obsolete on 16 August 1946.

Mark I*. Introduced 'for the record' and immediately declared obsolete in August 1946, this was a conversion of the Mk I to Mk IV standards. It is assumed to date from the early years of the Second World War.

Mark II (November 1915). This was simply a Mk I adapted for air service, with a spade grip and a two-tier magazine holding 97 rounds (approved in November 1916). The forced-draught cooling system was abandoned.

Mark II* (May 1918). This was an air-service conversion of the Mk I * approximating to Mk III standards.

Mark III (May 1918). A variant of the Mk I* offering a higher rate of fire, this incorporated modifications to the gas system.

British soldiers man a well-protected Lewis Gun defending a canal on the Western Front, 1917.

Mark IV. Apparently approved in 1938 – when BSA was given an order for 50,000 guns and 200,000 pan magazines – the true Mk IV Lewis Gun was based on a design originally promoted by the Soley Armament Company in the 1930s. It was officially introduced 'for the record' in August

1946 and immediately declared obsolete. The prototype was a stripped Mk I with a coil-pattern main spring in the butt, a Bren-type box magazine, and a monopod; production guns were apparently cannibalised from a mixture of old parts and new components.

Their most distinctive features are an elongated skeletal butt (attached to what had been the spade-grip frame) and an equally rudimentary pistol-grip/trigger guard unit. The helical mainspring was replaced by a coil spring contained in a tube extending from the back of the receiver to the butt plate. An angular gas-cylinder guard with a small hand-grip block lay beneath the barrel, and a crude bipod appeared beneath the leading edge of the magazine.

Wartime adaptations. Lewis Guns had been made in vast numbers during the First World War and, as supplies of replacement Bren Guns were only just appearing in 1939, were still serving with British forces. From the autumn of 1940 onward, efforts were made to refurbish existing Mk I ground guns and to convert obsolete aircraft guns for ground use. The quantities involved are not known with certainty, though Henry Atkin & Co., Parker-Hale, Westley Richards and Enfield delivered at least 58,000 of them. Atkin and Westley Richards then cannibalised 2,000 guns from old Mk II and Mk III aircraft guns, and a few were made from BSA-made components that had been in store since 1918. Guns also came from the USA (q.v.) under the Lend-Lease scheme.

Mk II and Mk III aircraft guns, plus many of their US .30 M1918 equivalents supplied under Lend-Lease, received rudimentary shoulder-stock extensions to the original spade grip – retained in its entirety – and crude fixed sights adjusted (theoretically) to a range of 400 yards. Early guns lacked mounts, but later examples had crude pressed-steel bipods. The changes appear to have been signified by the addition of a 'star' to the original designation (e.g., the Mk II aircraft gun became the Mk II* Land Service conversion, and the Mk I* became 'Mk I**').

'SS' pattern. Mk I (ground) guns were often modified to standards prescribed by the 'Gun, Machine, Lewis, 0.303-inch, Shoulder Shooting' ('SS'), approved for Naval Service in August 1942. The radiator assembly of the original ground guns was replaced by a cylinder guard and a short wood fore-end, the wood butt was shortened by 2 in, and a combination flash-hider/compensator was fitted to the muzzle. The guns had a distinctive monopod, and retained the original adjustable leaf sight.

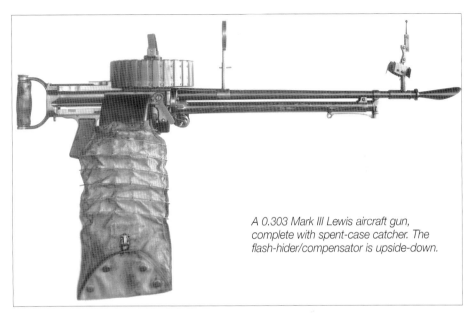

A 0.303 Mark III Lewis aircraft gun, complete with spent-case catcher. The flash-hider/compensator is upside-down.

Designation: Gun, Machine, Lewis, 0.303-inch Mark I
Made by the Birmingham Small Arms Company, Birmingham, England; and by the Savage Arms Company, Utica, New York State, USA

Specification: Standard infantry pattern
Data taken from Ian Hogg and
    John Weeks, Military Small Arms of the
    Twentieth Century, seventh edition,
    2000
Calibre: 7.7 mm (0.303 in)

Chambering: 0.303 in (7 x 56R)
Operation: gas; automatic fire only
Locking system: rotating bolt
Length: 1,283 mm (50.5 in)
Weight: 11.8 kg (26.0 lb)
Barrel: 666 mm (26.3 in), four grooves, left-hand twist
Mount: bipod
Feed system: pan, 47 rounds
Muzzle velocity: 745 m/sec (2,450 ft/sec) with standard Mk VIIZ ball ammunition
Cyclic rate: 550 rds/min

The 0.303 Hotchkiss Mark I, on its small 'cavalry' tripod. This is a tank gun with a detachable butt.

This was officially adopted in June 1916, largely because it was easier to make than the Vickers Gun. There is also a possibility that the Hotchkiss company, struggling to increase production of the M1914 for the French army, supplied surplus machinery to the British government.

Mark I. This had a wooden butt, with an integral pistol grip, an oil bottle and a hinged shoulder plate. It could only feed from conventional metal strips and was issued with a small 'cavalry' tripod. Light Hotchkiss guns fed from the right and were cocked by a bolt handle protruding from the back of the receiver above the pistol grip. The bolt handle doubled as a fire selector, depending on how far it was turned upward after cocking the gun; maximum cyclic rate was about 500 rds/min. Enfield-made guns had 'E'-prefix serial numbers.

Though the Hotchkiss was light enough to be carried forward with the infantry during an attack, its strip feed was inconvenient. This, together with worries about its reliability, confined the Hotchkiss to comparatively static roles. Renamed 'Gun, Machine, Hotchkiss, No. 2 Mk I*' in 1926, it remained in reserve for many years. After serving the Home Guard and the Merchant Navy during the Second World War, the Hotchkiss was finally declared obsolete in June 1946.

Mark I* (June 1917). Made for infantry (Mk I* No. 1) or tank use (Mk I* No. 2), these were identical except for the sights and butt fittings. No. 1 had a conventional tangent-leaf back sight offset on the left side of the feed cover, and a wooden butt with distinctive metal strengthening plates; No. 2 had a pistol grip adapted to take an optional tubular extension. Most tank guns were also issued with the 'Sight, Tubular, No. 2', a can for a 249-round cartridge belt – a series of articulated 3-round strips – and a bag to catch the ejected cases.

Indian troops pose with a Hotchkiss Gun. From a coloured postcard published by Raphael Tuck & Co. Ltd, c. 1915. Note the discarded gun shield (bottom right).

Designation: Gun, Machine, Hotchkiss, 0.303-inch Mark I
Made by the Royal Small Arms Factory, Enfield Lock, Middlesex

Specification: Standard pattern
Data taken from Ian Hogg and
   John Weeks, Military Small Arms of the
   Twentieth Century, seventh edition, 2000
Calibre: 7.7 mm (0.303 in)
Chambering: 0.303 in (7 x 56R)

Operation: automatic; gas
Locking system: rotating collar
Length: 1,187 mm (46.25 in)
Weight: 12.3 kg (27 lb) with bipod
Barrel: 596 mm (23.5 in), four grooves, right-hand twist
Mount: bipod
Feed system: metallic strips, 30 rounds
Muzzle velocity: 739 m/sec (2,425 f/sec) with standard Mk VIIZ ball ammunition
Cyclic rate: 500 rds/min

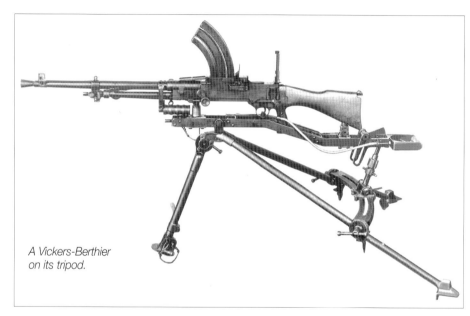

*A Vickers-Berthier
on its tripod.*

Patented prior to the First World War by the Frenchman Adolphe Berthier and issued in small numbers in Belgium, this gas-operated weapon was offered as a light machine-gun or a heavy automatic rifle. The US Army had been sufficiently impressed by the weapon to adopt it provisionally, but the First World War ended before series production could

begin and tests undertaken in 1919–20 were less encouraging.

Rights to the Berthier patents had been acquired in 1918 by Vickers, and development of a 0.303-calibre version, begun in 1922, had led to the perfection of the Vickers-Berthier ('VB') ground gun and its aircraft version, the Vickers Gas Operated ('VGO') by the late 1920s.

VB machine-guns took part in the British trials of 1930–1, but were unexpectedly beaten by the Czechoslovakian ZGB. However, though this Holek design was preferred by the army, deliveries from the Enfield small-arms factory would be delayed by creation of a new production line and would inevitably favour home-service units. As the situation in the Indian Army had become intolerable, owing to the unreliability of its obsolescent Hotchkiss and Lewis guns in hot and dusty conditions, the Vickers-Berthier was adopted for India Service in 1935.

I. Mark I. Resembling the Bren externally, this had a distinctive pistol-grip assembly. Three hundred were supplied from the Vickers factory in Crayford, Kent, in March 1936; 64 similar guns had gone to Iraq in 1935.

I. Mark II. This was an experimental gun distinguished by a slender butt, an unusually light barrel and panels milled out of the receiver. Though it weighed 3 lb less than the I. Mk I pattern, the Mk II was never adopted.

I. Mark III and **I. Mark IIIB.** Differing largely in barrel design and gas-plug arrangements, these derived from the Mk I and were made in the Ishapur rifle

The Vickers 'K' (or 'VGO') was an aircraft derivative of the Vickers-Berthier. This is an early gun, lacking the trigger arrangements of the perfected design.

factory from 1939 until work stopped early in 1942 so that tooling for the Bren Gun could begin.

VGO ('Vickers Gas Operated'). Known commercially as the 'Vickers K', this was a derivative of the Vickers-Berthier intended for Air Service, with a pan magazine and the mechanism altered to fire at 900 rds/min. The perfected guns also had a distinctive single spade grip with the trigger in a separate circular aperture. The VGO was installed on ring mounts and in some of the earliest gun-turrets to be fitted to British aircraft. When the Browning was preferred, and powered turrets replaced the open gun positions, displaced VGOs were offered to the British Army. There they were greatly favoured as vehicle guns, particularly as twin-gun installations were possible. Reliability in the desert commended them to the SAS and other mobile forces, and they served until 1945.

A belt-feed version was developed experimentally as the 'Vickers Central Action' (VCA), but was beaten by the Colt-Browning in RAF trials.

Designation: Gun, Machine, Vickers-Berthier, 0.303-inch, India Service Mark III
Made by the Ishapur rifle factory, India

Specification: Standard infantry gun
Data taken from Ian Hogg and
    John Weeks, Military Small Arms of the
    Twentieth Century, seventh edition,
    2000
Calibre: 7.7 mm (0.303 in)
Chambering: 0.303 in (7 x 56R)
Operation: selective; gas
Locking system: tilting bolt engaging the
    roof of the receiver
Length: 1,180 mm (46.5 in)
Weight; 9.4 kg (20.9 lb) without magazine
Barrel: 507 mm (23.9 in), five grooves,
    right-hand twist
Mount: bipod or tripod
Feed system: detachable box magazine,
    30 rounds
Muzzle velocity: 740 m/sec (2,425 ft/sec)
    with standard Mk VIIZ ball ammunition
Cyclic rate: 450 rds/min

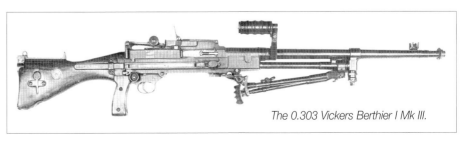

The 0.303 Vickers Berthier I Mk III.

Browning

Britain

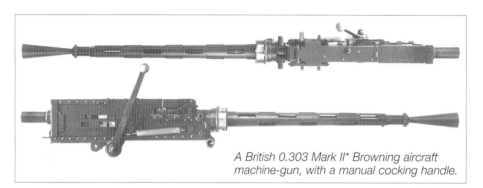

A British 0.303 Mark II* Browning aircraft machine-gun, with a manual cocking handle.

Renowned as the 'gun that won the Battle of Britain', the 0.303 Browning was the standard rifle-calibre weapon of the Royal Air Force. In 1934, after circulating a specification for a belt-fed aircraft gun to interested parties, the RAF had held a competition at Martlesham Heath. The Vickers Central Action ('VCA') gun proved to be efficient, but the testers decided that the Colt-Browning had more to offer. The War Department then negotiated suitable production licenses with Colt, and, in September 1935, contracts were placed with BSA and Vickers.

The British Browning, in addition to chambering the rimmed 0.303 round instead of the rimless 0.30 in pattern of the MG40, had an auxiliary sear system to hold the breech open after firing. By the end of 1939, BSA had made more than 27,000 guns, and had delivered more than 468,000 by the end of the war; Vickers did not participate in the manufacture of the Browning, owing to a conflict of priorities with the standard medium machine-gun. British Brownings were invariably found with slotted barrel casings and two-lever cocking assemblies on the receiver-side, though there was a wide range of mounts.

Mark I. Supplied by Colt in 1936–7, this was apparently a standard MG40 (later known as the 0.30 M2) chambering 0.303 cartridges, and could be adapted to accept the ammunition belt from either side of the feed block.

Mark I* and **Mark I****. Upgrades of the Mk I, these were distinguished by the addition of auxiliary sear units developed to prevent 'cooking-off' (ignition of chambered cartridges by heat alone) occurring after lengthy periods of rapid fire.

Mark II (1937). The perfected British-made gun had a new auxiliary sear system perfected by BSA.

Mark II*. This was a Mk II with a fluted muzzle collar and a finned flash-hider.

Designation: Gun, Machine, Browning, 0.303-inch, Mark I*
Made by BSA Guns Ltd, Birmingham, Warwickshire, England

Specification: Standard aircraft gun
   Approximate dimensions
Calibre: 7.7 mm (0.303 in)
Chambering: 0.303 in (7 x 56R)
Operation: automatic; short recoil
Locking system: vertically moving block entering the underside of the bolt
Length: 1,016 mm (40.0 in)
Weight: 10.7 kg (23.5 lb)
Barrel: 610 mm (24.0 in), four grooves, right-hand twist
Feed system: metal-link belt, 250 rounds
Muzzle velocity: 740 m/sec (2,425 ft/sec) with standard ball ammunition
Cyclic rate: 1,200 rds/min

The ZGB 4 was the final prototype of the Bren Gun.

Tests undertaken in the late 1920s and early 1930s showed that the Czechoslovakian ZB vz. 27 was preferable to the Vickers-Berthier, and a 0.303 version, the finalised ZGB, was approved for British service under the acronym 'Bren' (for Brno and Enfield). A production licence was signed on 24 May 1935.
Mark I. The first few guns of this type came from Brno in 1936, as the earliest deliveries of Enfield-made guns did not take place until September 1937. The order was completed in May 1939 with the assistance of BSA Guns Ltd. In October 1938, a supplementary order for 5,000 was given to Inglis, the first Canadian-made Mk I being test-fired in March 1940.

The first tripod mounts (copied from the ZB 206) came from Brno in November 1937, destined for India. They were successful enough to persuade the British authorities to place an order with BSA Guns Ltd in February 1939; more than 127,000 Mk I and Mk II tripods had been made by 1945, though most were destined to spend their lives in store.

When the war began in September 1939, Enfield had received orders for 15,512 Mk I Brens. Production was so slow and deliberate that the last guns from these pre-war contracts did not appear until 1942. The Bren was only just displacing Lewis Guns from front-line service when war began and the loss of vast quantities of equipment on the beaches of Dunkirk reduced the inventory to just 2130. This forced the British – fearing German invasion – immediately to

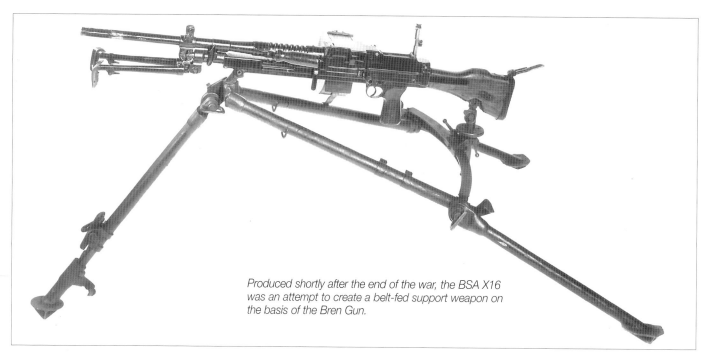

Produced shortly after the end of the war, the BSA X16 was an attempt to create a belt-fed support weapon on the basis of the Bren Gun.

impress obsolescent Lewis and Hotchkiss guns from store.

One answer was provided by the 'Monotype Scheme', an engineering syndicate led by Monotype & May Ltd. The idea was to disperse production so that air-raids were unlikely to entirely disrupt production. The principal participants were the Daimler Co. Ltd, the Hercules Cycle Co. Ltd, the Monotype Corporation Ltd,

Climax Rock Drill & Engineering Company, Tibbenham & Company, the British Tabulating Machine Co. Ltd and Sigmund Pumps Ltd. Each made only a few individual components, which were assembled in the Monotype factory near Redhill. When the war ended, the scheme had provided more than 80,000 guns.

Tooling had begun in the Toronto factory of the John Inglis Company in

1939, but production was still insignificant by the period of the Dunkirk evacuation. However, Inglis subsequently made about 120,000 0.303 guns for the Canadian and British forces, and about 43,000 7.9 mm guns for China. The total orders for Bren Guns (Enfield, Monotype and Inglis) amounted to about 417,000 from September 1939 and March 1944.

Bren Guns will be encountered on

three differing tripods: the original Mk I, with folding legs and an anti-aircraft adaptor; the simplified Mk II with fixed legs, introduced about 1941; and the lightweight Mk II* of 1944, intended for airborne troops. Among the special anti-aircraft mounts were the Motley cradle and the 'Gate', with guns suspended from overhead frames. The Lakeman Mount, a pendent system popular on armoured vehicles in 1940–1, had a large coil spring behind the support arm.

Even the earliest Bren Guns proved to be very efficient, but the magazines were troublesome. The basic design had soon proceeded from the Mark I to the perfected Mark II* by way of Marks I*, I*** and II. Total production of the .303 box magazines was approaching 10 million when the war ended. There were also two types of 100-round drum magazines, the Mark I being superseded by the Mark II, with a folding 'L'-shape winding handle. Production is said to have approached a million.

Mark I (Modified) (September 1940). This supplemented the pre-war Mk I and the Inglis made 'C. Mark I'. It had an angular (Mk I*) receiver, lacked the bracket for the optical sight, and the barrel-handle base became a simple welded tube. The butt slide (Mk II) was simplified and a new bipod (Mk II) was fitted. The Mk I Modified Bren was made only by Enfield in Britain, though some were subsequently made in Australia in the Lithgow factory. These have Australian Mk 3 bipods.

Mark II (June 1941). Made exclusively under the Monotype Scheme, this had a simpler body than the Mk I, a leaf-pattern back sight, a fixed cocking handle instead of the folding pattern, a simple stamped butt plate, a modified barrel with a detachable flash-hider/front-sight assembly, and a single recoil spring instead of two in the butt. The guns were originally made with Mk II bipods, but so many were repaired or altered at a later date that hybrids will be found. The 'C. Mark II' was similar, but had a distinctive Canadian-made variant of the Mk 3 bipod.

Mark 2/1 (1943). This was simply a 0.303 Mk II with a modified cocking handle and slide assembly, replacing the simplified fixed pattern developed in 1940.

Mark 3 (May 1944). This had a shorter barrel, a lightened receiver, simpler magazine-well and ejection-port covers, and a plain (Mark 4) butt. Mk I or Mk 3 bipods were standard.

Mark 4. Approved concurrently with the Mk 3 to conserve supplies of raw material, this had a modified Mk II-type barrel cradle, noticeably less metal in the receiver, and an ultra-short barrel with a new flash-hider.

Others. Experimental adaptations of the Bren made prior to 1939 included 7.92 mm DD/E/2143 ('Design Department, Enfield, drawing no. 2143'), developed to standardise ammunition with the Besa. This gun was hastily abandoned when the Second World War began, though trials had already shown great potential.

Designation: Gun, Machine, Bren, 0.303-inch Mark I
Made by the Československá Zbrojovka AS, Brno Czechoslovakia, the Royal Small Arms Factory, Enfield Lock, Middlesex and the John Inglis Company, Toronto, Canada

Specification: Standard infantry pattern
Data taken from Ian Hogg and
  John Weeks, Military Small Arms of the
  Twentieth Century, seventh edition,
  2000
Calibre: 7.7 mm (0.303 in)
Chambering: 0.303 in (7 x 56R)
Operation: automatic; gas
Locking system: tilting block engaging
  the roof of the receiver
Length: 1,150 mm (45.3 in)
Weight: 10.2 kg (22.3 lb) empty
Barrel: 635 mm (25.0 in), six grooves,
  right-hand twist
Mount: bipod
Feed system: detachable box magazine,
  30 rounds
Muzzle velocity: 730 m/sec (2,400 ft/sec)
  with standard Mk VIIZ ball ammunition
Cyclic rate: 500 rds/min

Besa Gun Britain

The British 7.92 mm Besa was popular as a vehicle gun. This is a Mark II, with selectable rates of fire.

Almost exclusively confined to armoured vehicles, this was another Czechoslovakian design. Offered to Britain in the mid 1930s and known commercially as the ZB 53 (militarily, as vz 37), it was a belt-feed air-cooled medium gun capable of sustaining fire over long periods. Credited to the Holek brothers, the gas-operated action was adapted from that of the vz. 26 but the concept of softening recoil was inspired by the Bren.

The Besa barrel was allowed to recoil. When the main spring returned the breech-block to battery, stripping a new round into the chamber, the barrel unit was released to move forward. As it did so, the gun fired and the recoil initially had to overcome the residual forward motion before reversing the action. The goal, achieved very successfully, was to reduce the stress transmitted to the gun mounting. The Besa soon attained an enviable reputation for smoothness and accuracy.

Development did not proceed as easily.

The first guns were delivered from the new BSA factory in Redditch in June 1939, but test-firing revealed so many problems that the gun had to be virtually re-engineered to work properly. Production was suspended until the spring of 1940. According to company records, BSA Guns Ltd made 59,332 7.92 mm Besas in 1939–46.

There was also a large-calibre Besa, chambered for a 15 mm cartridge, but this was derived from the ZB 60 instead of the ZB 53. Made only in comparatively small numbers, it was not as successful as the rifle-calibre versions and was declared obsolescent before the Second World War had ended. It was replaced by the 30 mm Aden cannon. Production amounted to merely 3,218 guns.

Mark I (June 1940). This had a selector lever (known as the 'accelerator') on the left side of the receiver giving 450 rds/min for general purposes and 750 rds/min for repelling close-range attacks.

Mark II (June 1940). Approved concurrently with the Mk I, this had a simplified receiver, a short barrel sleeve, a modified accelerator and a plain flash guard.

Mark II* (1941). These guns were basically Mk II made after the introduction of the Mk III.

They have the dual-rate fire system, but many of the components are simplified even though they usually interchange with earlier versions.

Mark III (August 1941). This gun lacked the selective fire-rate system, the fire-rate being fixed at 750 rds/min.

Mark III* (August 1941). This was a version of the Mk III restricted to 450 rds/min.

Designation: Gun, Machine, 7.92mm, Besa Mark I
Made by BSA Guns Ltd, Redditch

Specification: Standard pattern
Data taken from Ian Hogg and
    John Weeks, Military Small Arms of the
    Twentieth Century, seventh edition, 2000
Calibre: 7.92 mm (0.311 in)
Chambering: 7.92 x 57, rimless
Operation: automatic; gas
Locking system: tilting block engaging the
    roof of the receiver
Length: 1,105 mm (43.5 in)
Weight: 21.5 kg (47.0 lb)
Barrel: 736 mm (29.0 in), four grooves,
    right-hand twist
Mount: vehicle
Feed system: metal-link belt, 225 rounds
Muzzle velocity: 823 m/sec (2,700 ft/sec)
    with standard ball ammunition
Cyclic rate: 450 or 750 rds/min (selectable)

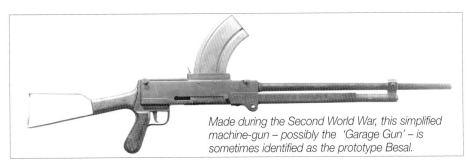

Made during the Second World War, this simplified machine-gun – possibly the 'Garage Gun' – is sometimes identified as the prototype Besal.

The ill-fated 0.303 Mk I Besal or Faulkner, adopted officially but never made in quantity.

The most Bren-like of the emergency designs was the Besal, formally approved in 1943 but never made in quantity. The prototype was demonstrated to the Small Arms Committee in March 1942, and subsequently underwent an encouraging trial. It seems to have had a skeletal butt and a fixed pistol grip beneath the rear of the receiver, and cocked by retracting a handle on the front right side of the breech.

A revised Besal, submitted in August 1942, was cocked by unlatching the pistol grip subassembly and pushing it forward to engage the bolt/piston extension unit, then retracting the components until the striker was held on the sear. This system was clearly inspired by the Besa, which had also drawn inspiration from Czechoslovakia. The improved Besal also had a two-position 'L'-type back sight, a simple bipod, and a carrying handle on the barrel.

Few problems were encountered during protracted testing in the winter of 1942 on the ranges at Pendine, so the Besal was adopted as the 'Faulkner' (the name of the designer). By the summer of 1943, however, the likelihood of a German invasion of Britain had passed. As deliveries of Bren Guns from Enfield, Inglis and the Monotype Scheme were more than adequate to meet existing demands, so the introduction of the Faulkner machine-gun was rescinded in June 1943.

Though the Besal operated much like a Bren and locked similarly, by displacing lugs on the bolt into the receiver wall, the return spring had been moved from the butt to a new location inside the piston extension.

Designation: Gun, Light, Machine, Faulkner, 0.303-inch
Made by BSA Guns Ltd, Redditch

Specification: Standard Mark I
Data taken from Ian Hogg and
    John Weeks, Military Small Arms of the
    Twentieth Century, seventh edition, 2000
Calibre: 7.7 mm (0.303 in)
Chambering: 0.303 in (7 x 56R)
Operation: automatic; short recoil
Locking system: block displaced upward
    into the receiver
Length: 1,185 mm (46.6 in)
Weight: 9.8 kg (21.5 lb)
Barrel: 558 mm (22.0 in), four grooves,
    right-hand twist
Mount: bipod
Feed system: detachable box magazine,
    30 rounds
Muzzle velocity: 745 m/sec (2,450 ft/sec)
    with standard Mk VIIZ ball ammunition
Cyclic rate: 600 rds/min

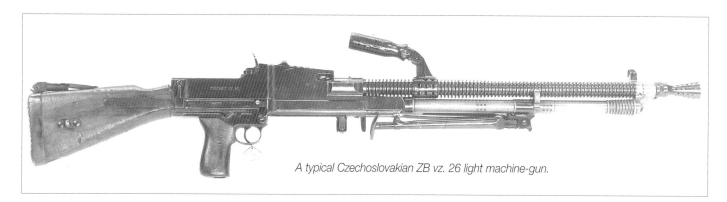

A typical Czechoslovakian ZB vz. 26 light machine-gun.

This gun originated in a design created in the early 1920s by Václav Holek for Zbrojovka Praga. Several years of development led to the Ruční Kulomet 'Praga' vz. 24 (Praga light machine-gun, model 1924), which amalgamated a top-mounted box magazine with the basic Praga I-23 action. The return spring ran back into the butt, and a specially sprung butt-plate was intended to absorb some of the recoil forces generated during prolonged firing.

By the time the prototypes had been perfected, a shoulder-support had been added to the butt, a drum sight had replaced the previous leaf, and the barrel had been partially finned to improve cooling. Successful tests against a Hotchkiss and a lightened Schwarzlose allowed the vz. 24 to be approved. But no sooner had field trials with the Czechoslovakian army begun than the Praga company collapsed. Production was switched to state-owned Zbrojovka Brno.

Once ZB technicians had made minor changes to facilitate mass production, the M24 became the vz. 26. Series production began immediately in Brno for the armed forces, but improvements in the bolt and gas system soon led to the vz. 27. The principal difference concerned the method of unlocking the bolt, which was achieved by cam tracks on the outside surface of the piston-rod extension (vz. 26), acting on the front of the breech-block, or by a cam surface on the piston post (vz. 27) acting towards the rear of the breech-block.

M26. The first series-made vz. 26 were delivered in 1928; by 1938, guns had been exported in quantity to Brazil, China, Ecuador, Iran, Japan, Lithuania and Yugoslavia. A few had also gone to Chile. All the guns were chambered for the Czechoslovakian 7.92 mm round, identical with the 7.9 x 57 mm German type, except the 7 x 57 examples sold to Brazil and Chile.

The vz. 26 and its successors were generally considered as light machine-

A 0.303 ZGB 30, showing the finned barrel and shortened gas-piston tube.

guns, though attempts were made to adapt them for support fire. However, though several impressive-looking tripod and quadrupod mounts were offered, limitations imposed by box magazines limited the volume of fire they could produce. The back sight was graduated only to 1,500 m, which distinguishes the 1926-type gun from the vz. 30.

M30. The Romanians, who had ordered the vz. 26 in quantity, indicated that they wished to make the guns under licence once a few changes had been made.

The resulting vz. 30 was similar externally to the vz. 26, but was marginally longer (1,180 mm compared with 1,165), had a seven-position adjustable gas-port assembly and a bolt/piston extension that differed greatly in construction. The back sight is graduated to 2,000 m instead of 1,500 m. Some guns will be encountered with a monopod beneath the butt, sliding radially in a special base plate.

By 1938, the vz. 30 had been exported in quantity to Afghanistan,

Bolivia, Ecuador, Ethiopia, Peru, Romania (where guns were subsequently made by CMC in Cugir) and Turkey; Guatemala, Latvia, Nicaragua and Uruguay had also purchased a few guns. More than 15,000 'M30' light machine-guns (vz. 30/J) were supplied to Yugoslavia in 1931–6, to be joined by 'M37' guns made in the government manufactory at Kragujevač, principally for the armed forces but also for limited export. The 7.92 mm cartridge was regarded as

The breech of the ZGB 30, showing the selector markings and the adjuster drum for the back sight.

standard, though 7 x 57 mm guns were supplied to Guatamela and Uruguay, and 7.65x53 mm examples to Bolivia and Peru.

ZGB 30 and 33. These were supplied to Britain in the 1930s, after the experimental vz. 27 had demonstrated its superiority over the Vickers-Berthier

(q.v.) in the British trials. The 0.303-calibre ZGB 30 Model 1 arrived in Britain in 1931, but proved to have too little power to extract and eject satisfactorily until the gas-tube had been radically shortened. The improved Model 2 (1932) also had its gas port closer to the breech, but the body and barrel assembly were allowed to slide back against a buffer to reduce apparent recoil. Then came the Model 3, with a new 30-round magazine and an attachment for an experimental 'tele-lensatic' sight.

The Model 4 (1934) had a shorter quick-detachable barrel, lacking the radiating fins of the preceding guns. The back sight lay on the receiver behind the magazine, and the rate of fire was reduced from 600 rds/min to 480 rds/min to reduce dispersion. The 'Improved Model 4' had a vertical back sight notch-plate and an folding handle beneath the butt to allow an underhand grip. Finally, 62 Improved Model 4 machine-guns were delivered early in 1935. They performed well enough in field trials to convince the British to adopt the ZGB, which became the Bren Gun (q.v.).

Brno also offered the 'ZGB vz. 30 commercially, selling them to Bulgaria (8 x 50R), Egypt, Iraq and Latvia (all 0.303). They could be identified by their cooling fins, as the finalised British ZGB 33 trials guns had plain barrels.

The ZGB 33 had a plain barrel.

Designation: Lehký kulomet ZB vz. 26
Made by Československá Zbrojovka AS,
Brno, Czechoslovakia

Specification: Standard infantry pattern
Data taken from Karl Fischer, Waffen-
und schiesstechnischer Leitfaden für
die Ordnungspolizei, 1943 edition
Calibre: 7.92 mm (0.311 in)

Chambering: 7.92 x 57, rimless
Operation: automatic; gas
Locking system: titling block engaging
the roof of the receiver
Length: 1,165 mm (45.9 in)
Weight: 9.0 kg (19.8 lb) without
magazine
Barrel: 602 mm (23.7 in), four grooves,
right-hand twist

Mount: bipod
Feed system: detachable box
magazine, 30 rounds
Muzzle velocity: 755 m/sec (2,475
ft/sec) with standard German sS ball
ammunition
Cyclic rate: 600 rds/min

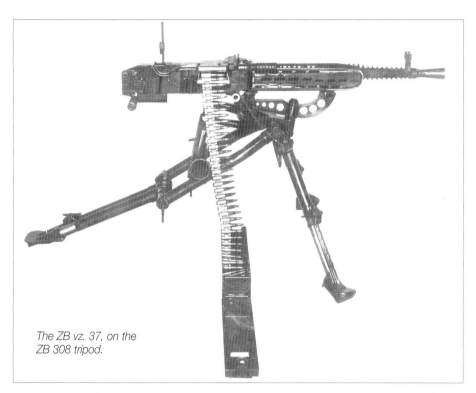

*The ZB vz. 37, on the
ZB 308 tripod.*

Miroslav Ročik, but this proved to be unsatisfactory. It was succeeded by the gas-operated ZB 52, which was capable of dual rates of fire and allowed the gun to fire while the moving parts were still returning to battery. Tests suggested a variety of minor improvements, and a few ZB 53 guns were delivered for trials in November 1934. These were successful enough for the 'tezhký kulomet vz. 35' to be adopted for military service.

A few hundred guns were supplied for what were effectively extended field trials, and others were sold to Iran and Romania. However, experience suggested improvements, and the vz. 35 was superseded by the vz. 37 at the end of 1936. Probably only about 1,000 1935-type machine-guns had been made, and were classed as 'non-interchangeable'. The perfected vz. 37 was accompanied by a 'vz. 37' tripod (known commercially as ZB 308), which was ultimately found to be unnecessarily complicated; a simpler ZB 309 was developed as a replacement, but not issued in quantity until after the Second World War had ended.

The vz. 37 (still often known commercially as the 'ZB 53') was made

As the Schwarzlose blowback system (see 'Austria-Hungary') was only marginally strong enough for the 7.9 mm cartridge, attempts were made to

transform the Holek Praga I-23 design into a suitable heavy machine-gun. The first stage was the recoil-operated ZB 50, developed by Václav Holek and

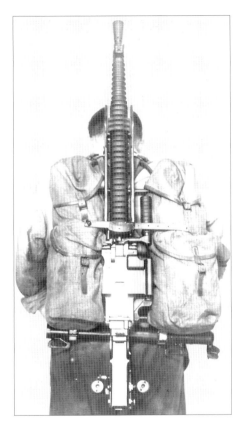

Man-packing the ZB vz. 37.

in three versions. The standard infantry pattern had spade grips and was accompanied by the tripod; the tank or

A typical ZB vz. 37 mounted on the simplified post-war ZB 309 tripod.

vehicle gun, vz. 37 UV, had a pistol grip and a shoulder stock; and the version intended for fortresses and strong-points (vz. 37 O) appears to have had a special pintle mount. The largest purchaser of these guns was Romania, which acquired 6,500 infantry and 1,470 fortress guns; other large-scale orders went to China and Iran, and 14 infantry and 453 vehicle guns were purchased for trials in Britain. These led to a licence to make the 'Besa' (q.v.), production being entrusted to BSA Guns Ltd. Afghanistan, Chile, Peru, Slovakia and Yugoslavia all purchased ZB 53 in small quantities.

The Germans also seized the guns that were in store in 1939, issuing them as 'schwere Maschinengewehre 37 (t)'. Production was moved from Brno to

Vsetin in 1941, but gradually declined as the facilities were put to making parts for the standard German machine-guns.

Designation: 7.92 mm tezhký kulomet ZB vz. 35
Made by Československá Zbrojovka AS, Brno and Vsetin, Czechoslovakia

Specification: Standard infantry pattern
Data taken from Ian Hogg and
John Weeks, Military Small Arms of the Twentieth Century, seventh edition, 2000
Calibre: 7.92 mm (0.311 in)
Chambering: 7.92 x 57, rimless
Operation: automatic; gas
Locking system: tilting block engaging the roof of the receiver
Length: 1,105 mm (43.5 in)
Weight: 18.6 kg (41.0 lb)
Barrel: 678 mm (26.7 in), four grooves, right-hand twist
Mount tripod
Feed system: metal-link belt, 100 or 200 rounds
Muzzle velocity: 792 m/sec (2,600 ft/sec) with standard ball ammunition
Cyclic rate: 500 and 750 rds/min (selectable)

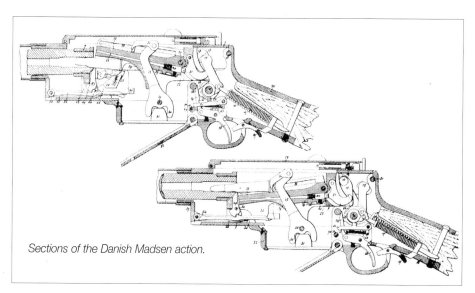

Sections of the Danish Madsen action.

Patented by Jens Tørring Schouboe in 1902, this was a clever adaptation of the Peabody breech system. Adopted by the Danish army, initially as a cavalry weapon (carried in a saddle scabbard in the same way as a carbine), the guns were still being made in the 1950s by Dansk-Industri-Synikat AS ('DISA-Madsen'), which had succeeded Dansk-Rekylriffel-Syndikat ('DRSD') in 1936 – in virtually the same form as the original pattern!

Unusually, the action is recoil-operated. Most of the successful light machine-guns of comparable size and weight have been gas-operated, yet the Madsen was still out-performing them in competitive trials as late as 1939. In Brazil in 1935, for example, the Danish gun had beaten a variety of Browning, Colt, Hotchkiss, Vickers and ZB designs in the light machine-gun category and the concurrent search for a heavy-support gun. This was

very unusual, particularly as the Madsen was air-cooled, but the figures make interesting reading. In some trials, the superiority was extremely obvious.

It is possible that the Madsen action was less sensitive to variations in ammunition than gas-operated rivals, yet the Browning and the Vickers Guns (both recoil-operated) failed miserably in Brazil. Another factor may have been chambering. Madsens were never adopted officially for anything other than small-scale use, but the manufacturer successfully sold them throughout south and central America and the Far East. Development work had been undertaken with virtually every service round, rimmed and rimless alike, and the explanation may simply be that Madsen had solved problems linked with chambering, pressure, and the timing of the operating cycle that was unique to each cartridge.

The Madsen did not emerge from the Russo-Japanese War with much credit, being withdrawn from the Russian cavalry owing to claims that it jammed excessively, and the Austro-Hungarian experiences during the First World War were also unhappy. However, there is evidence that the guns performed better in the fighting than the Russians claimed; in an all-day skirmish at Nan-chen, in March 1905, six

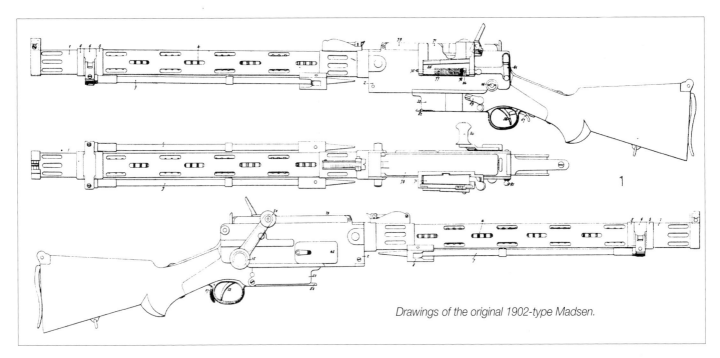

Drawings of the original 1902-type Madsen.

1

Madsens fired between 27,700 and 39,600 rounds (reports vary!) without any breakages and only a handful of stoppages. The Austro-Hungarian guns were altered from 6.5 mm to 8 x 57 mm in Vienna, and were never satisfactory.

However, there is evidence to show that the Madsen, well though it performed under trial conditions, was susceptible to jamming in mud. The guns supplied to France were rapidly replaced by the CSRG ('Chauchat'), which was undeniably a backward step, and the British also encountered problems with Madsens being tested as tank guns. Both armies used rimmed cartridges, which were probably responsible for at least some of the problems.

When the Madsen fires, the barrel, barrel extension and breech-block are allowed to recoil within the receiver until a stud on the underside of the breech-block comes to the end of the short horizontal section of a closed cam path. The stud then rises, lifting the breech-block around a pivot at the rear, and then runs back along the upper part of the cam plate. At the limit of its backward movement, just as the stud is ready to descend, the barrel is released to run forward. The spent case is extracted and

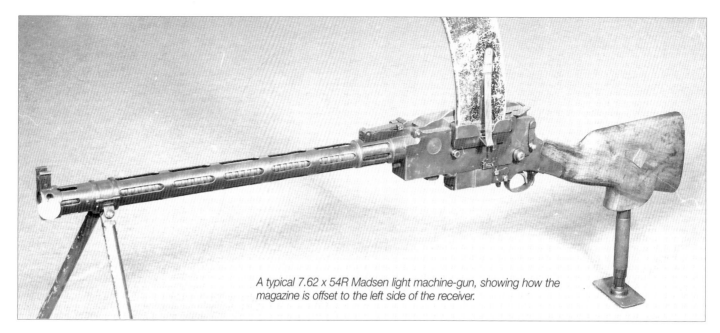

A typical 7.62 x 54R Madsen light machine-gun, showing how the magazine is offset to the left side of the receiver.

falls out of the bottom of the receiver. Driven by the return spring, the breech-block is then lowered to receive a cartridge in its grooved upper face, runs forward to allow the cartridge to be rammed into the breech, and is then raised to return to battery and align the firing pin with the chamber.

Externally, the guns were conventional. They fed from a detachable box magazine on the left side of the breech, allowing centreline sights to be fitted, and the barrel was protected by a sheet-steel jacket. Most guns had bipods and wooden butts, often with provision for a monopod, though tripods were made to allow fire to be sustained. Most of the guns made prior to 1920 could fire single shots, but many later patterns were restricted to automatic fire. Markings on the left side of the receiver will usually identify the purchaser, though virtually each delivery was given a 'Model designation' that was actually the year of purchase.

There is no evidence that the many 'models' differed greatly from each other in any respects other than chambering, sights and butt arrangements. However, some had exceptionally short barrels (475 mm), with the back sight on top of the receiver alongside the magazine, and the latest or M1950 Madsen had an accelerator to boost the cyclic rate from 450 to 600 rds/min.

Rexer. These guns were advertised by the Rexer Arms Company of London, licensee of Madsen rifles and machine-guns for the 'United Kingdom and the Dominion of

Canada'. Rexer failed to honour the agreement by attempting to sell guns elsewhere, forcing DRS to recover guns and machinery in 1909, but the Madsen gun was still often known as the 'Rexer' in Britain prior to 1918.

Designation: 8 mm let Maskingevaer Madsen Modell 1902
Made by Dansk Rekylriffel Syndikat AS

'Madsen', Copenhagen, Denmark
Specification: Standard cavalry pattern
Data taken from Pierre Lorain, 'La Gageure du Lieutenant Schouboe', in Gazette des Armes (May 1978)
Calibre: 8 mm (0.315 in)
Chambering: 8 x 58, rimmed
Operation: selective; recoil
Locking system: reciprocating breech-block
Length: 1,120 mm (44.1 in)

Weight: 7.5 kg (16.5 lb) with bipod, but no magazine
Barrel: 587 mm (23.1 in), four grooves, right-hand twist
Mount: bipod
Feed system: detachable box magazine, 25 rounds
Muzzle velocity: 610 m/sec (2,000 ft/sec) with standard ball ammunition
Cyclic rate: 450 rds/min

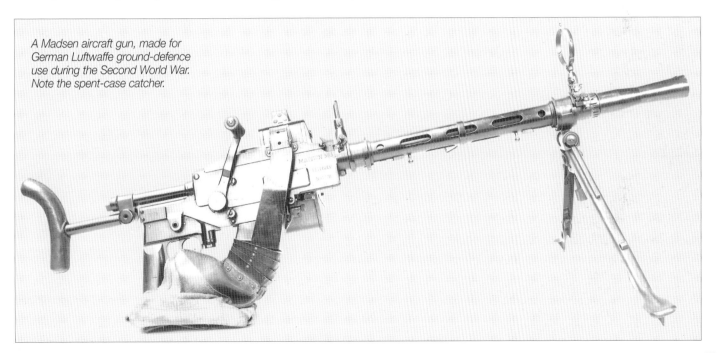

A Madsen aircraft gun, made for German Luftwaffe ground-defence use during the Second World War. Note the spent-case catcher.

Hotchkiss M1900 France

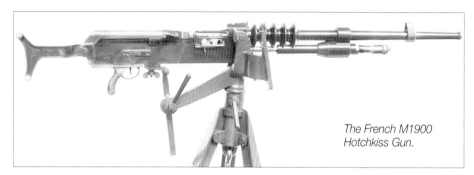

The French M1900 Hotchkiss Gun.

The original Hotchkiss machine-gun – a manually operated multi-barrel gun similar externally to the Gatling – had been invented by an American, Benjamin Berkley Hotchkiss, in the 1870s. No sooner had this weapon had been eclipsed by the Maxim than Hotchkiss et Cie was approached by an Austrian inventor, Adolf von Odkolek zu Augezd. Odkolek had been granted a series of patents in 1890–3 to protect a gas-operated machine-gun, but had been unable to arouse interest in his native country.

The Hotchkiss management immediately saw the potential of the Odkolek gun, and acquired rights from the inventor on the harshest possible terms. By the mid 1890s, the Odkolek had become the Hotchkiss and the inventor was all but forgotten.

The gun was perfected in 1895–6 and introduced in 1897, when it was offered in a variety of chamberings. Compared with a recoil-operated Maxim, the Odkolek system was very simple. Gas was tapped from the bore, about two-thirds of the way to the muzzle, and allowed to strike a piston that was formed as part of the carrier. When the gun fired, gas pressure thrust the piston/carrier back and cam surfaces on the carrier raised the locking struts (pivoted on the tail of the bolt) out of engagement with seats in the receiver walls. This allowed the bolt and carrier to run back to the limit of recoil; simultaneously, a cam-track in the piston extension acted with a pawl to move the next cartridge into place. As the return spring pushed the bolt and the piston-carrier unit forward, a new round was pushed into the chamber.

Hotchkiss machine-guns fed from distinctive metal strips, which allowed the cartridges to be pushed forward into the chamber – unlike the Maxim, which had to retract each round backwards and align it with the breech mechanically. Hotchkiss guns fed rimless ammunition efficiently, particularly if the cartridges were parallel-sided, but rimmed taper-body cartridges such as the French 8x51 or British .303 presented more of a problem.

The earliest or 1897-pattern guns were offered in 'light' and 'heavy' patterns, the former with a plain cylindrical barrel and the latter with four large-diameter fins intended to present greater surface area to the atmosphere and enhance cooling. Mounts ranged from simple fixed-leg tripods (Affût trépied Mle. 97), with provision for neither mechanical elevation nor traverse, to wheeled carriages with armoured shields.

Trials showed that the Hotchkiss was the first gun to combine simplicity with reliability, and the French army bought a small batch in 1897. Others were soon being sold abroad. The design was constantly improved (though usually only in minor respects). The

An early attempt at combining machine-guns and motor traction. This 1903-vintage photograph shows a Hotchkiss Gun mounted on a lightly armoured car. Note the tripod secured to the bodywork.

French government then produced the 'M1905' – a dismal failure – and then the M1907 (Saint-Étienne), which lost much of the original inspiration. However, neither of the 'improved' French guns proved successful. When the First World War began, the French, as short of machine-guns as the British, ordered huge quantities of the perfected M1914 from Hotchkiss to supplement the Saint-Étienne.

The first gun to be purchased in quantity by the French army, more than 200 M1900 examples were still emplaced in fortifications or in store in 1914. They were similar to the 1897-type guns, but the gas system was improved. The gas tube had originally been full-length, drilled with radial gas-escape holes, but was prone to clogging. The new tube was a half-length open-ended design with a 20-position gas regulator, which was so sensitive that a chart was issued with each gun correlating ambient temperatures with regulator settings. The cocking handle was changed from a hook beneath the action to a handle on the left side of the receiver, the barrel fins (usually five) were cast into a bronze collar around the barrel, and a radial safety lever was added to the left rear of the receiver. French-issue guns had tangent-leaf sights on top of the receiver above the bronze feed block, but others (sometimes called 'Mle 02' or 'Mle 03') had a sight that was elevated by a knurled finger-wheel protruding obliquely from the receiver behind the feed block.

1900-type guns were sold to Japan in 6.5 x 50; to Norway, Portugal and Sweden in 6.5 mm; to Brazil, Chile and Mexico in 7 x 57; to Belgium and Bolivia in 7.65 mm; to China in 8 x 57, and to New Zealand in 0.303. The guns featured in Engineering in 1903 included a rate regulator; there was also a large-calibre version, chambered for a 0.472 in (12 mm) cartridge developing 2,020 ft/sec (616 m/sec), which fed from 20-round strips. The text claims that the large Hotchkiss was developed as a result of experience in the South African or Boer War (1899–1902), when the range of the rifle-calibre guns had proved insufficient.

M1905 (Puteaux). A modification of the basic Hotchkiss credited to government technicians in the Puteaux factory (APX, 'Ateliers de Puteaux'), this could be distinguished by the squared contours of the breech (very similar to the later Saint-Étienne), small-diameter fins that ran half the length of the barrel, and a return spring that was concentric with the barrel from the cooling fins to a collar at the muzzle. The gas port was moved to the muzzle, and a fire-rate adjuster was introduced. This was theoretically capable of altering the rate from eight to 650 rds/min. The changes to the barrel were expected to improve cooling, but proved to be little other than a trap for oil and dirt. When any prolonged firing was undertaken, not only did the barrel overheat but a haze of oil vapour disturbed the sight picture.

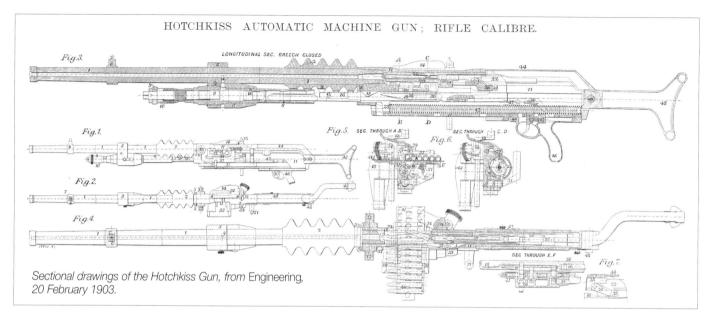

HOTCHKISS AUTOMATIC MACHINE GUN; RIFLE CALIBRE.

Sectional drawings of the Hotchkiss Gun, from Engineering, *20 February 1903.*

The APX retained Hotchkiss-style feed strips, but these were not interchangeable with the original form – particularly unfortunate, as 1900-type Hotchkiss guns were serving with the cavalry and in the colonies. The mount was either the 1900-type Hotchkiss tripod or the M1905 quadrupod, with distinctively curved legs.

The troublesome 1905-type guns were rapidly withdrawn from the field army and relegated to static use in fortresses and strong-points, where the drawbacks were not so obvious.

Designation: Mitrailleuse Hotchkiss
Made by Société Anonyme des anciens établissements Hotchkiss et Cie, Saint-Denis

Specification: 'M1903' rifle-calibre gun
Data taken from Engineering, 20 February 1903 (figures marked '*' from 3 April 1897)
Calibre: 'any between 6 mm and 8 mm'
Chambering: various rimmed, semi-rim and rimless rounds
Operation: automatic; gas

Locking system: pivoting struts on the bolt engaging the receiver walls
Length: 1,360 mm (53.5 in)*
Weight: 23.0 kg (50.6 lb)
Barrel: 825 mm (32.5 in)*, four grooves, left-hand twist
Mount: tripod (17.9 kg, 39.5 lb),
Feed system: metallic strip, 30 rounds
Muzzle velocity: 600–750 m/sec (1,970–2,460 ft/sec), depending on ammunition
Cyclic rate: 100 (low rate) or 500–600 rds/min (high rate)

Saint-Étienne M1907　　　　　　　　　　　　　　France

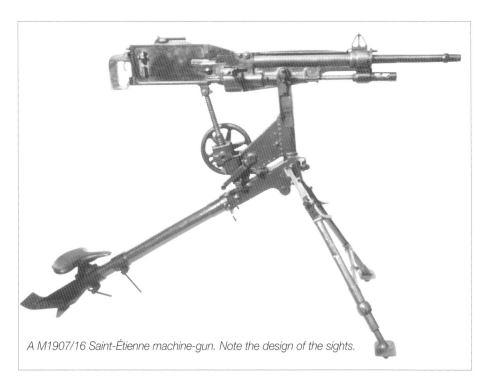

A M1907/16 Saint-Étienne machine-gun. Note the design of the sights.

This was a French government design, credited to technicians in the Saint-Étienne ordnance factory, that reached the troops in 1909. The inspiration was provided by the Hotchkiss, but a variety of changes was made in a quest for a more battleworthy weapon. Not all of these were advantageous, and the Saint-Étienne has had more than its fair share of critics.

Though potentially an improvement on the Hotchkiss in several respects (most notably the detachable barrel), the toggle-joint lock and the operating mechanism were grave mistakes. This may have been intended to reduce the recoil effect, a praiseworthy goal, but forced the designers to introduce a rack, pinion and cam-plate mechanism to reverse the motion and open the breech. The return spring, inside the lower rear of the receiver in the original Hotchkiss, was exposed to heat and dirt beneath the barrel. Retaining metallic-strip feed was also unwise, particularly as they could not interchange with the Hotchkiss design (the Saint-Étienne withdrew cartridges backwards before raising them in line with the chamber), and the incorporation of rate-regulators showed that little had been learned from the Puteaux gun of 1905. The Saint-Étienne not only had a lever on the rear left side of the breech to select 'high' or 'low' fire-rates, but also had a regulator knob to vary the rate within each of the two basic categories. This theoretically allowed a cyclic rate of 10–600 rds/min.

The M1907 had a streamlined appearance, with a slender barrel and a single handgrip attached to the receiver back plate. A tangent sight, inspired by the

A French gun-crew with its Saint-Étienne M1907/16.

German Lange design, lay on top of the breech. The standard mount was either the Affût-trépied 1907 C, or the M1915 'Type Omnibus'. However, a special forked pillar was made in small numbers for trench service; when used in this way, the guns were fitted with a butt extension instead of a spade grip.

M1907/16. Combat experience revealed the shortcomings of the basic design, and an improved version was substituted. A new gas-pressure regulator was fitted, the firing pin was changed, and a distinctive 2,400m back sight, with a dial-type base, replaced the original tangent-leaf type. However, the

modified machine-gun was not much of an improvement on its predecessor. Though thousands were made, output peaking at about 1,900 monthly from September 1916 to January 1917, the decision was taken to concentrate on the Hotchkiss and work on the Saint-Étienne declined rapidly after May 1917. By May 1918, monthly deliveries were averaging only about 50 guns. Many Saint-Étiennes were scrapped after the Armistice, post-1920 survivors being despatched to the French colonies.

Designation Mitrailleuse Modèle 1907, dit 'Saint-Étienne'
Made by Manufacture Nationale d'Armes de Saint-Étienne

Specification: Mle 1907
Data taken from Jean Huon, Un siècle d'armement mondial, tome 3, 1979
Calibre: 8 mm (0.315 in)
Chambering: 8 x 51, rimmed
Operation: automatic; gas
Locking system: toggle joint
Length: 1,180 mm (46.5 in)
Weight: 23.8 kg (52.5 lb) without mount
Barrel: 710 mm (28.0 in), four grooves, left-hand twist
Mount: tripod, 32.7 kg/72.1 lb (M1907)
Feed system: metallic strip, 25 rounds
Muzzle velocity: 700 m/sec (2,300 ft/sec) with standard ball ammunition
Cyclic rate: 600 rds/min (max.)

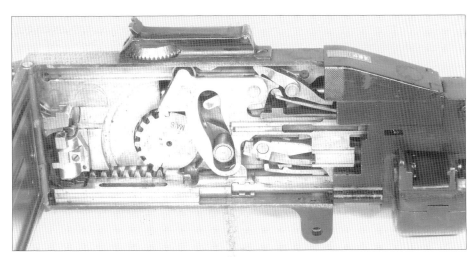

The breech of the M1907/16 Saint-Étienne, showing the complexity of the mechanism required to convert the forward motion of the piston rod to the rearward movement of the breech-block.

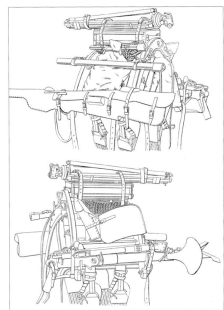

These drawings (left and right-side views) show how a scabbarded Saint-Étienne machine-gun, tripod, ammunition-box, rangefinder and rangefinder tripod were carried on a single pack-saddle.

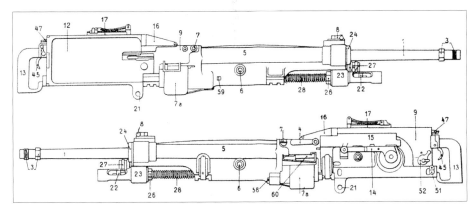

Drawings of the M1907 Saint-Étienne, showing the original sights.

Hotchkiss M1908   France

Known commercially (and to the US Army) as the 'M1909' or Portative, this was designed by Laurence Benét and Henri Mercié. It relied on a locking collar ('fermeture nut'), containing an interrupted screw, which engaged threads on the bolt to lock the action. The feed was inverted so that cartridges lay underneath the strip, the idea apparently being to protect them from rain. However, the strips were much more difficult to load than the standard type. Indeed, so awkward was the feed that rumours arose in the USA (where the 'Machine Gun Rifle, Caliber .30, Model of 1909' was serving in small numbers) that the gun could only be fired in daylight.

The French adopted the light Hotchkiss as a cavalry weapon in 1908, with a 2000m tangent-leaf back sight, but it was too large and heavy for this role. A few changes were made to the sights and the bipod in 1913, creating the so-called 'M1908/13', but surviving guns were replaced by the Lewis or the infamous Chauchat during the First World War – though not before a few had been used in the air. Hotchkiss guns were also fitted in many of the first French tanks. The earliest guns were

fed with 25-round strips, sometimes linked to form a rudimentary 100-round belt, but belts made of 25 3-round striplets were eventually substituted.

It seems that production had ceased by 1914, and that the French government was committed to developing other designs – particularly the execrable Chauchat – that were suited to a doctrine of assault-at-the-walk. Consequently, Hotchkiss was allowed to sell remaining guns to Britain. As the Hotchkiss was much easier to make than the Vickers or Maxim, rights were purchased and a production line installed in the Royal Small Arms Factory at Enfield (see above).

Guns of this type had also been sold to Belgium (in 7.65 x 53) and Sweden (6.5 x 55), and ex-British 0.303 examples were used in Mexico.

Designation: Fusil Mitrailleur Hotchkiss, Modèle 1908 ('Hotchkiss Portative')
Made by Société Anonyme des anciens établissements Hotchkiss et Cie, Saint-Denis

Specification: Standard French cavalry pattern
Data taken from Jean Huon, Un siècle d'armement mondial, tome 3, 1979
Calibre: 8 mm (0.315 in)
Chambering: 8 x 51, rimmed
Operation: automatic; gas
Locking system: pivoting struts on the bolt engaging the receiver walls
Length: 1,190 mm (46.9 in)
Weight: 12.5 kg (27.6 lb) with bipod
Barrel: 565 mm (22.2 in), four grooves, left-hand twist
Mount: bipod, with an optional monopod beneath the butt
Feed system: metallic strip, 30 rounds
Muzzle velocity: 650 m/sec (2,130 ft/sec) with standard ball ammunition
Cyclic rate: 500 rds/min

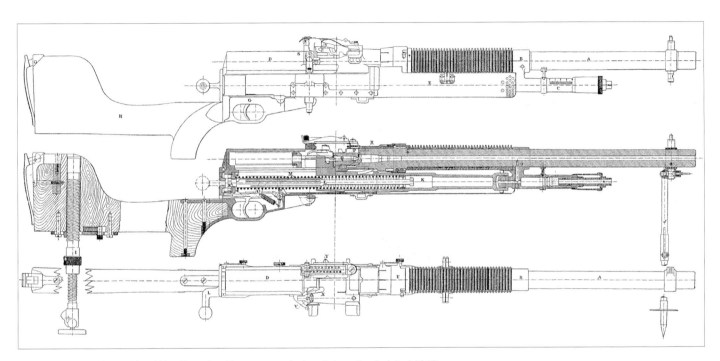

Drawings of the M1908 Hotchkiss Portative. From a manufacturer's handbook dated 1910.

The M1914 8 x 51R Hotchkiss was a sturdy and dependable gun that served the French until the Second World War.

The perfected version of the basic Odkolek/Hotchkiss design, this served the French army in great quantity during the First World War. Though it was very similar externally to the preceding guns, it had steel fins on the barrel. The feed block and the pistol grip were still bronze castings, but the feed was refined, the safety catch of the 1900-type guns was abandoned and the regulator was restricted to four positions instead of twenty. Most guns were mounted on the M1914 or M1916 Hotchkiss tripods, though the M1907 and M1915 Omnibus mounts could be used if adaptors were available.

The M1914 Hotchkiss, accepted by the French army only because the First World War had begun, was sturdy and reliable. A well-trained crew could sustain fire for surprisingly long periods, as long as care was taken not to damage the feed strips. Fortunately, the mechanical strip-filling machine also re-set any of the cartridge-holding fingers than had been bent over. The only other problem arose from ammunition; the guns were initially restricted to the Balle 1886 M, as the primers of the older Balle 1886 D were unsatisfactory. The introduction of 1886 D AM ammunition, with different primers, corrected the problem.

The first deliveries were made to the French army in December 1914, production rising to about 1,400 monthly by February 1917 and peaking at about 2,000 monthly in July 1918. The reliability of the Hotchkiss contrasted with the poor performance of the Saint-Étienne, and the M1914 was still the preferred front-line machine-gun in 1940. Most of the guns had been given 2400m dial-elevated sights, which had been approved in 1932. They were also sometimes accompanied by the M1928 anti-aircraft adaptor, which

A French Hotchkiss gun-crew take a break from supporting British soldiers.

fitted on to the tripod to elevate the gun to shoulder height.

Balloon Gun. This was an enlarged version of the M1914, inspired by the old 13.2 mm-calibre guns. Chambered for 11 mm Gras ammunition, loaded with incendiary bullets, it was intended to bring down the German observation and artillery-spotting balloons that customarily rose out of rifle range behind the front line. The success of the large-calibre machine-guns is said to have inspired development of the .50 Browning.

M1930. Inspired by the Balloon Gun, this enlarged and modernised form of the M1914 was intended for a variety of uses. Locked by the well-tried flap system and chambering a 13.2 x 99 mm round, the M1930 had a single spade grip and a barrel that was

finned in its entirety, though there were three diameters. It was about 1,660 mm (65.4 in) long and weighed 39.7 kg (87.5 lb). Feed was either a 15-round metal strip or a 25-round detachable box magazine. Cyclic rate was about 450 rds/min. Mounts ranged from sturdy tripods to wheeled and shielded mounts for heavy support and anti-tank roles, to pillar mounts for anti-aircraft defence aboard small warships. Some guns were also used in aircraft.

Large-calibre Hotchkiss guns of this type were sold to Chile, China, Mexico and Romania. They were also made under licence by Breda in Italy (as the 'Mo. 1931'), and in Japan as the Type 93.

M1935. The 13.2 mm cartridge had the same case-length as the 0.5 Browning

round (12.7 x 99), and so, owing to the potentially fatal chance of accidentally using the wrong ammunition, Hotchkiss decided to shorten the case to 96 mm. The M35 was a minor variant of the original gun, chambering the new cartridge. The change in dimension was small enough to prevent wholesale changes in the gun.

Designation: Mitrailleuse Hotchkiss Modèle 1914
Made by Société Anonyme des anciens établissements Hotchkiss et Cie, Saint-Denis and Lyon

Specification: M1914 infantry pattern
Data taken from Jean Huon, Un siècle d'armement mondial, tome 3, 1979
Calibre: 8 mm (0.315 in)
Chambering: 8 x 51, rimmed
Operation: automatic; gas
Locking system: pivoting struts on the bolt engaging the receiver walls
Length: 1,310 mm (51.6 in)
Weight: 23.5 kg (51.8 lb)
Barrel: 785 mm (30.9 in), four grooves, left-hand twist
Mount: tripod, 24.0 kg/52.9 lb (M1916 pattern)
Feed system: metallic strip, 24 rounds (infantry), or 249-round articulated strip (tanks)
Muzzle velocity: 700 m/sec (2,295 ft/sec) with standard ball ammunition
Cyclic rate: 600 rds/min

CSRG (Chauchat) M1915   France

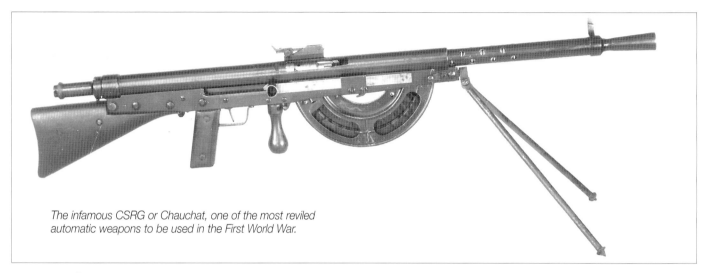

The infamous CSRG or Chauchat, one of the most reviled automatic weapons to be used in the First World War.

If the Saint-Étienne machine-gun was a poor design, this was only barely combat worthy. The CSRG or 8 mm Chauchat Machine Rifle had origins that dated back prior to the First World War and was ordered into production in September 1914. Designed by Chauchat, Sutter and Ribeyrolles, the gun was specifically intended to be made in poorly equipped factories. Consequently, the contract was given to one of France's leading bicycle-making

businesses, Établissements des Cycles 'Clément-Gladiator'.

Unfortunately, the combination of comparatively light weight and long-recoil action, moving backward greater than the length of the cartridge, made the gun impossible to control. The bolt and barrel ran back together. At the end of the stroke, the bolt was held while the barrel returned, following to strip a new cartridge into the chamber and re-lock the action. The design of many individual parts was

crude, and there were large surfaces to rub together and ultimately wear down.

Trials have suggested that only the first round ever hit an individual target, the second and subsequent shots flying surprisingly wide of the mark. The Chauchat was also notoriously prone to breakages.

Though Gladiator may have had unrivalled experience of metallic-tube fabrication, what was suitable for a bicycle was rarely appropriate for a machine-gun.

A French poilu *demonstrates how to fire a CSRG. The gun was notoriously difficult to shoot accurately and required a strong grip with both hands.*

In addition, the unique semicircular magazine was badly designed and the sharply tapering 8 x 51 rimmed cartridges jammed regularly. One French authority offered the opinion that it was rare for a Chauchat to fire a 20-round magazine without at least one stoppage.

The gun is easily identified, owing to its tube-like layout. The wooden butt is tacked on to the housing beneath the tube, and a pistol grip protrudes between the trigger guard and the magazine. A spindly bipod is attached beneath the barrel casing.

In addition to the thousands used by the French army, the CSRG served in Belgium and Greece. The Greek guns were usually listed as '7.8 mm

Gladiators', but still chambered the regulation French 8 mm ammunition. Others are said to have been sent to Poland in the early 1920s. Some guns remained in French service after the end of the First World War, the last being withdrawn from colonial forces in Morocco in 1932.

M1918. The US Army acquired nearly 13,000 standard 8 mm French M1915 machine rifles, and then asked for the design to be altered to accept the .30 M1906 round. Though the rimless cartridges promised to feed more efficiently, and a short straight box magazine could be substituted for the semi-circular French design, the new gun was a disaster. The American ammunition was much more powerful than the French 8 mm type, and strained construction that was already weak to its limits. Though 25,000 '0.30 Chauchat Automatic Rifles' were ordered, so many case-head separations and parts breakages ensued that some men refused to fire them. Only about 2,200 were issued for training purposes; survivors were scrapped soon after the Armistice.

Designation: Fusil Mitrailleur CSRG, Modèle 1915
Made by Établissements des Cycles 'Clément-Gladiator', Paris

Specification: Standard pattern
Data taken from Jean Huon, Un siècle d'armement mondial, tome 3, 1979
Calibre: 8 mm (0.315 in)
Chambering: 8 x 51, rimmed
Operation: automatic; long recoil
Locking system: rotating bolt head
Length: 1,170 mm (46.1 in)
Weight: 10.45 kg (23.0 lb) with loaded magazine
Barrel: 450 mm (17.7 in), four grooves, left-hand twist
Mount: bipod
Feed system: detachable box magazine, 20 rounds
Muzzle velocity: 600 m/sec (1,970 ft/sec) with standard ball ammunition
Cyclic rate: 240 rds/min

Darne M1918 France

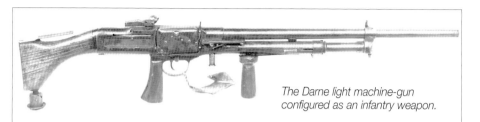

The Darne light machine-gun configured as an infantry weapon.

The Darne brothers' gunmaking business was recruited to make Lewis Guns for the French armed forces in 1916, though facilities that had been devoted to sporting guns were unable to make more than a few machine-guns weekly. Eventually, Régis Darne designed a gun of his own but only a few seem to have been made prior to the Armistice. They were subcontracted to Unceta y Cia to prevent disrupting work on the Lewis Guns.

The Darne was a compact gas-operated weapon with a tipping-block breech mechanism. The design of the locking piece was particularly clever, as it was cammed into engagement with the receiver by the breech-block; no separate carrier or piston-rod extension was needed. Belt feed was standard.

Initially conceived as an aircraft observers' gun, to replace the Lewis, the 1918-pattern Darne was supplied to the French air service at the end of the First World War; a few lightweight examples were delivered to the army, as machine rifles (Fusils mitrailleur), but fighting ceased before they could be issued and the contracts were cancelled. However, the M1930 went in quantity to the French naval air force (in wing, turret and synchronised versions) and the army used the M1933 as a tank gun. The aircraft guns were to be replaced by Brownings, but the Second World War began before progress could be made.

Darne guns were used in quantity in Brazil, Lithuania, Spain and Yugoslavia, and tested extensively in Britain and Czechoslovakia.

The machine-rifles and the light (Portative) and heavy ground guns usually had superfluous rate regulators, but the aircraft and tank guns had a fixed rate of 1,000–1,350 rds/min (depending on individual design). A large-calibre Darne was also sold in small numbers, firing .50 Browning or 13.2 mm Hotchkiss rounds at about 900 rds/min.

Designation: Mitrailleuse Darne
Made for R. & P. Darne, Saint-Étienne, by Unceta y Cia, Guernica, Spain

Specification: ground-service 'Portative' pattern
Data taken from Jean Huon, Un siècle d'armement mondial, tome 3, 1979
Calibre: 8 mm (0.315 in)
Chambering: 8 x 51, rimmed
Operation: automatic; gas
Locking system: tilting breech-block engaging the roof of the receiver
Length: 1,100 mm (43.3 in)
Weight: 9.0 kg (19.8 lb) without mount
Barrel: 660 mm (26.0 in), four grooves, left-hand twist
Mount: bipod (0.8 kg/1.8 lb) or tripod (13 kg/28.7 lb)
Feed system: fabric belt, 250 rounds
Muzzle velocity: 700 m/sec (2,295 ft/sec) with standard Balle 1886 M ammunition
Cyclic rate: 150–1,000 rds/min (variable)

Hotchkiss M1922 — France

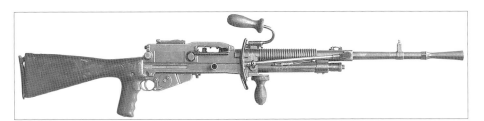

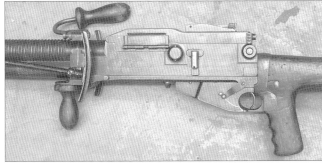

A 1922-type Hotchkiss light machine-gun, made in France for Turkey in the 1920s.

The French authorities purchased a few 'M1934' light machine-guns, with strip feed. Chambered for the 7.5 x 54 rimless cartridge, these were sent to serve in Indo-China. They were eventually replaced by the M24/29 'machine rifle'.

Designation: Mitrailleuse légère Hotchkiss Modèle 1934
Made by Société Anonyme des anciens établissements Hotchkiss et Cie, Saint-Denis

This was a modernised form of the 1914-type Hotchkiss, retaining the basic gas-operated flap-locked action altered by the inclusion of links. However, it was offered with a form of belt feed, using jointed metallic striplets, or with a detachable box magazine on top of the receiver. The guns had distinctive pistol-grip butts, bipods with noticeable 'rocker' feet, and flash-hiders that were cut obliquely to serve as compensators. The cocking slide lay on the right side of the breech.

Guns of this type – advertised as the 'M1924', 'M1926 or 'M1934' – were exported in small quantities. Purchasers included Greece and Romania (6.5 mm); Brazil, Chile, the Dominican Republic and Spain (7 x 57); Lebanon (7.5 x 54) and China (7.9 x 57). A few 0.303 adaptations were tested unsuccessfully in Britain against the Vickers-Berthier, and about 1,000 7.92 x 57 guns went to Czechoslovakia for field trials against the prototype ZB vz. 26.

Specification: French colonial infantry pattern
Data taken from Jean Huon, Un siècle d'armement mondial, tome 3, 1979
Calibre: 7.5 mm (0.295 in)
Chambering: 7.5 x 54, rimless
Operation: automatic; gas
Locking system: pivoting struts on the bolt engaging the receiver walls
Length: 1,216 mm (47.9 in)
Weight: 9.58 kg (21.1 lb) with bipod
Barrel: 600 mm (23.6 in), four grooves, left-hand twist
Mount: bipod
Feed system: metallic strip, 30 rounds
Muzzle velocity: 860 m/sec (2,820 ft/sec) with standard Balle 1929 C ammunition
Cyclic rate: 450 rds/min

Châtellerault M1924   France

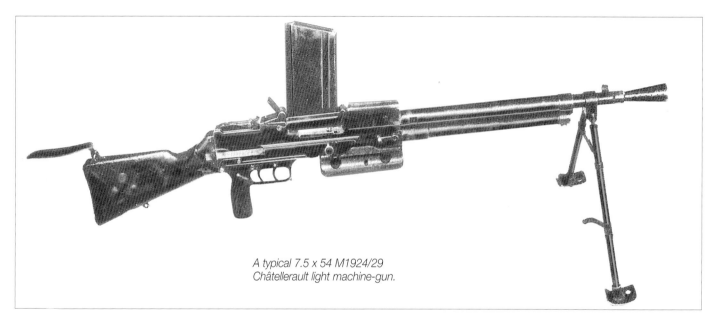

*A typical 7.5 x 54 M1924/29
Châtellerault light machine-gun.*

The performance of the French machine-guns during the First World War had left so much to be desired, particularly when compared with the German Maxim and the British Vickers, that it was clear by 1918 that better equipment was needed. Though economics dictated that the Mle 07/16 T Saint-Étienne should be retained, work began to develop a new light machine-gun.

Trials were undertaken during the early 1920s with a variety of designs, including the Madsen, the light Hotchkiss, the Lewis Gun, the Browning Automatic Rifle and the Berthier. These were joined in 1922 by the MAS 22 (a copy of the BAR) and then in April 1923 by the MAC 23. The MAC 23 soon outperformed the BAR and the MAS 22, and the Berthier, designed by a

Frenchman, was rejected by a government reluctant to pay royalties to Vickers-Armstrongs.

The new gas-operated gun, officially adopted as the Fusil Mitrailleur Modèle 1924 and issued to the troops from 1926 onward, bears a vague externally affinity with the Czech vz. 26 or the British Bren Gun, but has a distinctive double trigger

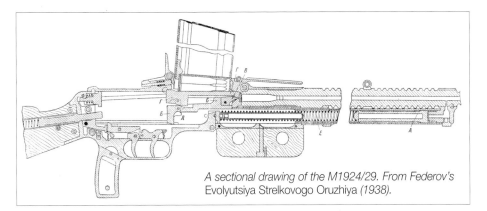

A sectional drawing of the M1924/29. From Federov's Evolyutsiya Strelkovogo Oruzhiya *(1938).*

and a short wooden fore-end. The action was an adaptation of the Hotchkiss relying on a swinging Colt-Browning link to tip the tail of the bolt up against a recess in the receiver. A top-mounted box magazine was fitted, and the only quirky feature was the use of a double-trigger firing system. The front trigger, which embodied a disconnector, gave single shots; the rear trigger, which held the sear and sear buffer down, allowed automatic fire.

The M1924 proved to be sturdy and efficient, and was an immense improvement on the Chauchat. However, it was unnecessarily complicated: there were 164 parts (excluding the magazine), including a variety of pins and no fewer than 21 springs. Comparable figures for the Japanese Taisho 11th year gun of 1922, also a Hotchkiss derivative, were 61

and 6; the Soviet DP of 1927 had merely 53 components, ten being springs.

Though the M1924 was easily field-stripped, the barrel-change system was poor. Not only did the barrel screw into the receiver, but it carried the bipod and lacked a handle. In addition, the gas-cylinder tube had to be detached before the barrel unit could be removed.

M1924/29. No sooner had production begun, however, than problems with the new rimless 7.5 mm cartridge arose. The dimensions of the case were so similar to the German 7.9 mm cartridge that accidents had occurred, and so a decision was taken to shorten the 7.5 mm version by 4 mm. The result was the 7.5 mm Balle 1929 C, and the guns that had been chambered for the original were returned to the ordnance factories for

revision. Many M1924/29 were rifled and sighted for 1933-type heavy-bullet ammunition, which performed far better at long-range than the standard type; these guns have barrels marked with a large 'D'. The machine-guns remained in production until the end of the Second World War and lasted in front-line service into the 1960s. Most of those that were on the inventory in 1940 were issued to Vichy forces and police.

Designation: Fusil Mitrailleur Modèle 1924 ('F.M. 24')
Made by Manufactures Nationale d'Armes, Châtellerault and Saint-Étienne

Specification: Standard M1924/29
Data taken from Jean Huon, Un siècle
    d'armement mondial, tome 3, 1979
Calibre: 7.5 mm (0.295 in)
Chambering: 7.5 x 54, rimless
Operation: automatic; gas
Locking system: displacement of the
    breech-block into the roof of the receiver
Length: 1,070 mm (42.1 in)
Weight: 8.93 kg (19.7 lb) without magazine
Barrel: 500 mm (19.7 in), four grooves,
    left-hand twist
Mount: bipod
Feed system: detachable box magazine,
    25 rounds
Muzzle velocity: 780 m/sec (2,560 ft/sec)
    with standard Balle 1933 D ammunition
Cyclic rate: 450 rds/min

Châtellerault M1931   France

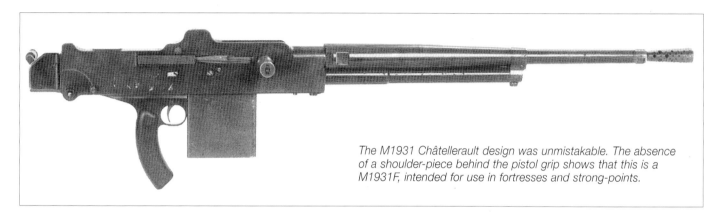

The M1931 Châtellerault design was unmistakable. The absence of a shoulder-piece behind the pistol grip shows that this is a M1931F, intended for use in fortresses and strong-points.

This shared the action of the perfected Mle 24/29 infantry gun (and is sometimes considered as a derivative), but the method of firing was different and there was little commonality of parts.

Credited to Commandant Riebel, leader of the design team, the M1931 ('MAC 31') was a heavy-barrel gun intended to fulfil a variety of roles. Consequently, it was made in a bewildering variety of similar, but by no means identical patterns. Production was continued after 1940 under German auspices, most post-1942 guns bearing the code 'jwh' allocated to the Châtellerault factory.

The M1931 cannot be mistaken for any other design. It has a tapering barrel, with neither fins nor flutes, and a squared receiver with a cocking slide. A large squared ejection chute lies directly beneath the feed port, and the pistol grip – uniquely – curves forward. Most guns were fitted with a drum magazine, which engaged a spindle projecting from the side of the receiver, but a short horizontal box magazine was also developed. Some, though not all guns, had a shoulder pad attached to the underside of the receiver back-plate.

Surviving guns of virtually any type were sent to equip the Atlantic Wall,

built by the Germans on the northern coast of France during the Second World War.

M1931 C. This was a tank (Char) gun. It could be identified by the aluminium shoulder piece (13cm deep) and a short ejection chute. Feed could be left- or right-hand, with the cocking slide on the opposite side. Flash-hiders were standard, but the sights were generally mounted independently elsewhere in the vehicle. Some guns were converted for ground service in 1940, receiving bipods and strut-like butts. Most also had carrying handles on the receiver.

M1931 E. Essentially similar to the M31 C, this had a 480 mm barrel instead of the standard 600 mm pattern, which brought the muzzle back almost as far as the gas port.

M1931 F. Developed specifically for service in fortifications (Fortresses) and strong-points, notably the Maginot Line, this was made to be used in 'paired' form and could feed from the left or the right. The charging handle was extended backward and the ejection chute was much deeper than the tank-gun patterns. No shoulder piece was fitted. Some guns were fitted with a cooling system, relying on the injection of water into the chamber after each shot. This was intended to allow fire to be sustained and extend the life of the barrel. Most guns were rifled for the heavyweight 7.5 mm Balle 1933 D, which ranged farther than the standard Balle 1924 C.

M1931 T and TM. These were essentially similar guns intended for use in remote installations. They lacked pistol grips and shoulder pieces, and were adapted to special mounts. The ejection chutes were curved so that ejected cases were directed outward beneath the magazines. The charging handle was straight, and the guns were fired with Bowden cables. The 'T' was supported from below and the 'TM' from above. The latter also lacked the ejection chute.

M1934 A. Intended to be used in aircraft wings (ailes), this relied on a shortened gas-path, a shorted recoil stroke, a lightweight bolt/carrier assembly, and an accelerator (a secondary function of the 'amortisseur de culasse') to raise the fire-rate to 1200 rds/min. Owing to the great weight of the special 300-round drum magazine, a pinion protruding from a housing on the base of the receiver rotated a rack on the periphery of the magazine. The guns had two safety devices, one mechanical and one pneumatic. Charging and firing were also accomplished pneumatically. The M1934 A was mounted on its left side, allowing the axis of the magazine to be vertical and ejected cases to fall through the ejection port.

M1934 T. Another of the aircraft guns, this was installed in turrets (tourelles). It lacked the power-drive feature of the M1934 A, and fed from non-rotating drums. Charging was accomplished manually, though firing was controlled by a Bowden cable.

M1934/39. Made only in small quantities, this belt-feed adaptation of the basic design was intended to replace the complex and unreliable M1934 A. The belt was a metallic-link pattern that allowed the cartridges to be rammed directly into the chamber. However, very few guns of this type had been made when the Germans invaded France in 1940.

Designation: Mitrailleuse de Fortresse Modèle 31 ('MAC 31 F')
Made by Manufacture Nationale d'Armes, Châtellerault

Specification: standard M1931 F
Data taken from Jean Huon, Un siècle d'armement mondial, tome 3, 1979
Calibre: 7.5 mm (0.295 in)
Chambering: 7.5 x 54, rimless
Operation: automatic; gas
Locking system: displacement of the breech-block into the roof of the receiver
Length: 1,050 mm (41.3 in)
Weight: 10.7 kg (23.6 lb) without magazine, 18.47 kg (40.7 lb) with loaded magazine
Barrel: 600 mm (23.6 in), four grooves, left-hand twist
Mount: see text
Feed system: detachable drum, 150 rounds
Muzzle velocity: 800 m/sec (2,625 ft/sec) with Balle 1933 D ammunition
Cyclic rate: 500 rds/min

Maxim M1908   Germany

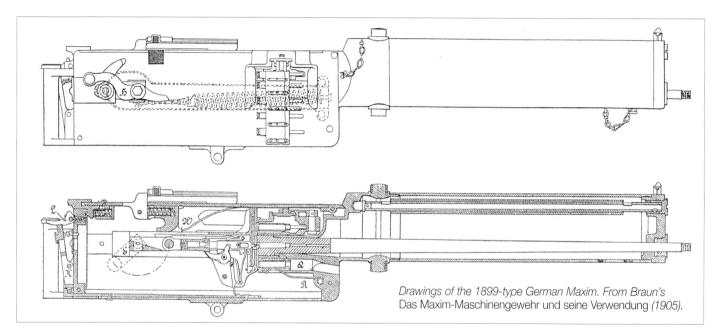

Drawings of the 1899-type German Maxim. From Braun's Das Maxim-Maschinengewehr und seine Verwendung *(1905).*

The Maxim, originating in the 1880s, had excited the interest of many armies. German had purchased a few in 1896, mainly for naval use, and then issued small numbers of MG. 99 and MG. 01 for field-service trials before adopting the MG. 08'. A production licence had already been granted by Vickers, Sons & Maxim to

Deutsche Waffen- & Munitionsfabriken, and the rifle factory at Spandau delivered the first government-made guns in 1910.

The barrel and breech-block of the MG. 08 ran back through about 17mm, securely locked together, until the barrel stopped and a locking toggle broke downward to allow the breech-block to run back alone.

After withdrawing a new round from the fabric feed belt on the rearward stroke, the mechanism returned to re-load. The toggle than snapped back into place and the main spring pushed the barrel/breech assembly back to its initial position.

The gun operated reliably, but the cyclic rate of the earliest guns was only about

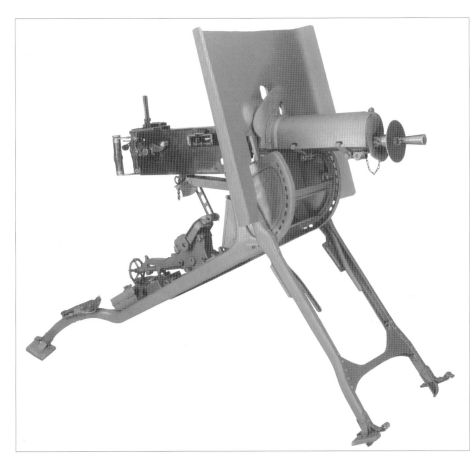

A typical MG. 08 Maxim, on its sledge mount. Shields of this type were rarely issued in German service; this one may originate in Turkey. Note also the armoured mantlet protecting the barrel jacket.

300 rds/min. Experience of trench warfare suggested that this was too slow to halt large-scale attacks, and a recoil booster ('Rückstossverstärker S.') was developed to increase the fire-rate to about 450 rds/min simply by deflecting propellant gas to increase the rearward thrust on the barrel. A few guns – particularly those being used on aircraft – were altered during the First World War (aptierte Art, 'altered pattern') to accept Austrian Keller-Ruszitska disintegrating-link belts in addition to the standard fabric pattern.

Only about 2,000 Maxims were available in August 1914, but wartime production was spectacular. The Inter-Allied Military Control Commission ordered the destruction of all but four of 87,950 machine-guns collected together in 1919! Few changes were made to the Maxims during the Weimar Republic, apart from the addition of anti-aircraft sights, adapting the back sights for heavy ball ammunition, modifying the feed for canvas or metal-link belts, and adding limit-stops and trajectory tables on the Schlitten 08.

Model 1909. This designation was applied to a variant of the MG. 08 offered for sale commercially. Guns of this type were distinguished by their mounts, which were conventional tripods instead of military-style sledges. Few orders seem to have been placed prior to 1914, except on behalf of Turkey (q.v.), though a few

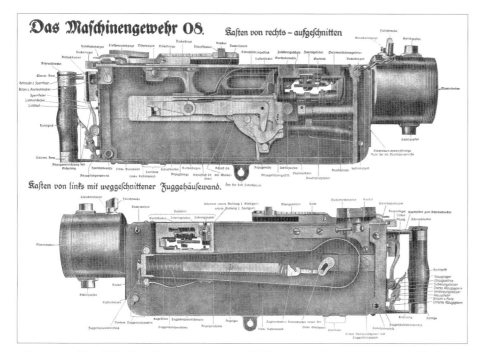

The parts of the MG. 08 action, from Fischer's Waffen- und schiesstechnischer Leitfaden für die Ordungspolizei (1944).

A British soldier examines an abandoned German MG. 08 Maxim, on a small static mount.

A German gun-crew, pictured during the Weimar Republic, man their MG. 08.

guns may have gone to South America in 7 x 57 and 7.65 x 53.

MG. 08/15. The MG. 08 was heavy and cumbersome, weighing about 26.5 kg, and the perfected sledge mount (Schlitten 08) contributed an additional 32 kg. When the first Lewis light machine-guns were captured on the Western Front, the Gewehrprüfungskommission ('G.P.K.') immediately refined the basic Maxim into a more mobile weapon. Credited to Oberst von Merkatz of the G.P.K., the MG. 08/15 had a small-diameter barrel jacket, thinner receiver walls than the MG.08, a new pistol grip and butt, a bipod and a simpler back sight.

Weighing nearly 18 kg, the MG. 08/15 was much more cumbersome than the Lewis or the Madsen. However, being water-cooled and based on well-tried

The MG. 08/15 was a clumsy 'light machine-gun', an expedient that retained belt feed and water cooling.

components, it was more reliable and could sustain fire much more effectively than air-cooled rivals that tended to overheat if used too enthusiastically.

MG. 16. A belated attempt had been made during the First World War to develop a simplified machine-gun for universal ground use (the so-called Einheitsmaschinengewehr 16), but development of this water-cooled adaptation of the MG. 08/15 was abandoned in 1917 to prevent interfering with production of the regulation patterns. The only tangible result of the Einheitsmaschinengewehr programme was the adoption of the tripod, or Dreifuss 16, as a substitute for the Schlitten 08.

Aircraft guns. These were made in several forms, ranging from air-cooled versions of the MG. 08 (with slotted barrel casings) to special versions of the MG. 08/15, usually designated 'MG. 08/18'. These could be identified by the shape of the receiver, which had a notable step behind the feed block, and by the small-diameter slotted barrel casings. Many were used in conjunction with synchronisation gear, and had sturdier springs and auxiliary buffers in an attempt to raise cyclic rate.

Designation: Maschinengewehr Modell 1908 ('MG. 08')
Made by Deutsche Waffen- & Munitionsfabriken (marked with a DWM monogram) in Berlin; the government rifle factories in Erfurt and Spandau; Rheinische Metallwaaren- & Maschinenfabrik ('Rh.M.& M.F.') in Sömmerda; Siemens & Halske ('S.& H.') in Berlin; and Maschinenfabrik Augsburg-Nürnberg ('M.A.N.').

Specification: Standard MG. 08
Data taken from John Walter, Central Powers' Small Arms of World War One, 1999
Calibre: 7.9 mm (0.311 in)
Chambering: 7.9 x 57, rimless
Operation: automatic; short recoil
Locking system: toggle mechanism, breaking downward
Length: 1,095 mm (43.1 in) without muzzle booster
Weight: 26.5 kg (58.3 lb) empty
Barrel: 720 mm (28.4 in), four grooves, right-hand twist
Mount: sledge, 32.5 kg (71.7 lb)
Feed system: fabric belt, 100 or 250 rounds
Muzzle velocity: 860 m/sec (2,820 ft/sec) with standard ball ammunition
Cyclic rate: 300 rds/min without booster

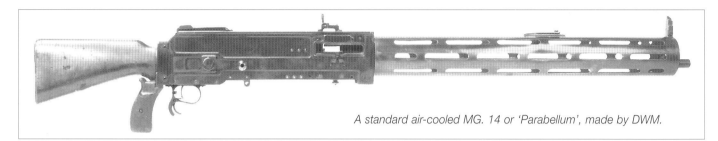

A standard air-cooled MG. 14 or 'Parabellum', made by DWM.

This was a lightened version of the Maxim, similar to the Vickers Gun. The principal change concerned the toggle mechanism, which was altered to break upward. In addition, the return spring, placed externally on the left side of the Maxim receiver, was moved to a tube protruding from the back plate inside the wooden butt. Consequently, the Parabellum, or 'Schweres Maschinengewehr M1913' ('S. M. Gew. M. 1913', was much lighter than the MG. 08 and had a shallower receiver. Changes were also made in the action, and a conventional pistol-grip/trigger assembly was attached to the rear lower edge of the receiver.

The Parabellum was widely used as an aircraft gun, mounted on pillar or ring mounts and fed with belts supported in a drum or reel. Known as the 'Modell 1914' in military service, most guns were air cooled and had slotted barrel jackets. Those issued to the Zeppelins, however, were water-cooled to prevent the chance of a hot barrel igniting hydrogen vented from valves in the top surface of the giant airships.

M1914/17. Similar mechanically to the M1914, this could be distinguished by the small-diameter barrel casing with a rudimentary carrying handle and a bipod bracket under the muzzle. Most were used in the air, though some guns were pressed into ground service during the spring offensives of 1918.

Designation: leichtes Maschinengewehr Parabellum, Modell 1914
Made by Deutsche Waffen- & Munitionsfabriken, Berlin-Charlottenburg and Berlin-Wittenau

Specification: standard air-cooled M1914
Data taken from John Walter, Central Powers' Small Arms of World War One, 1999
Calibre: 7.9 mm (0.311 in)
Chambering: 7.9 x 57, rimless
Operation: automatic; short recoil
Locking system: toggle mechanism, breaking upward
Length: 1,225 mm (48.2 in)
Weight: 10.2 kg (22.4 lb)
Barrel: 705 mm (27.8 in), four grooves, right-hand twist
Mount: pintle
Feed system: fabric belt, 100 or 200 rounds
Muzzle velocity: 860 m/sec (2,820 ft/sec) with standard ball ammunition
Cyclic rate: 600–650 rds/min

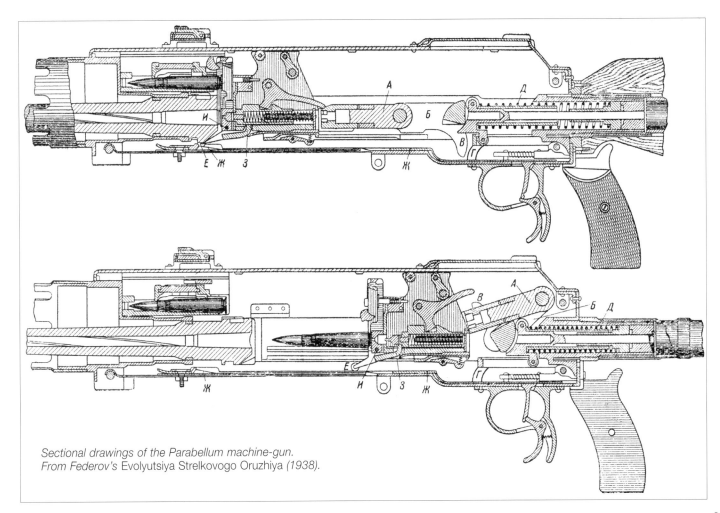

Sectional drawings of the Parabellum machine-gun.
From Federov's Evolyutsiya Strelkovogo Oruzhiya *(1938).*

Bergmann and Dreyse

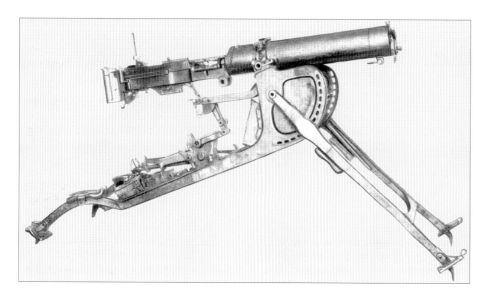

These guns, with pedigrees that stretched back some years, were both ordered into series production in 1915 to supplement the stocks of MG. 08. Both were recoil-operated and water-cooled, and were adapted to fit the Schlitten 08.

Made by Theodor Bergmanns Industriewerk, the Bergmann had been patented in 1902–5 by Louis and Hugo Schmeisser and made in small numbers without ever persuading the German army that it was a better prospect than the well-established Maxim. It used 'push-through' metal link belts and fed from right to left. The Dreyse, designed in 1908–9 by Louis Schmeisser for Rneinische Metallwaaren- & Maschinenfabrik, had had a similar lack of success.

The principal differences lay in the locking system. The Bergmann relied on a hollow locking block in the barrel extension that was cammed vertically out of engagement with the bolt; the Dreyse had a rocking strut that engaged the tail of the bolt. Both were much more compact than the Maxim toggle system – particularly the Bergmann – but lacked the durability of their rival. The Dreyse strut-lock, similar to some early Mannlicher pistols, was a poor design.

The feed systems were also different from the Maxim. The Bergmann relied partly on mechanical movement and partly on springs, and the Dreyse had a pawl driven by recoil. Though both worked well enough when in good repair, neither had great reserves of power in adverse conditions.

Consequently, though the Bergmann-MG. 15 was made in some numbers, most were sent to Turkey once the Germans realised that production of MG. 08 and MG. 08/15 was exceeding expectations. Production of the Dreyse-MG. 15 seems to have been meagre, though the basic locking system was

The Bergmann M1915 nA light machine-gun, showing the shoulder pad, pistol grip and minuscule tripod. These began life as aircraft weapons, but were withdrawn after belt-feed problems arose.

revived in the post-war MG. 13 (q.v.). Rheinische Metallwaaren- & Maschinenfabrik had soon been ordered to make the MG. 08 instead.

L. MG. 15. This was the Bergmann design adapted to provide an aircraft gun suitable for fixed forward-firing installations. Lighter and much more compact than the Maxims, desirable characteristics in an aircraft gun, the Bergmann seemed ideal – until pilots began to report that it jammed too frequently to be trusted in combat. The problem was soon traced to the spring-assisted return stroke of the feed mechanism, which malfunctioned if the aircraft was turning sharply to the left. No time could be spared to rectify the design fault, and the Bergmanns were withdrawn from air service. Many were re-issued as ground guns, with rudimentary shoulder pads attached to the back plate, a pistol-grip/trigger assembly beneath the receiver and crude sights. A protective sheet-steel guard could be pivoted down to cover the feed aperture, and the slotted sheet-steel barrel jacket had a carrying handle. The guns were issued in conjunction with a minuscule tripod.

M1915 Bergmanns were made in two patterns – old ('a.A.', alter Art) and new ('n.A.', neue Art), differing in the action. The former fired from an open bolt, but accuracy had proved to be poor; the latter, therefore, reverted to closed-bolt operation. Both fed from the right. They were handier in the light role than the cumbersome MG. 08/15, but the design of the butt and the tripod prevented firing from the prone position.

Designation: leichtes Maschinengewehr Bergmann, Modell 1915
Made by Theodor Bergmann, Abteilung Waffenbau, Suhl, Thüringen

Specification: l. MG. 15 n.A.
Data taken from John Walter, Central Powers' Small Arms of World War One, 1999
Calibre: 7.9 mm (0.311 in)
Chambering: 7.9 x 57, rimless
Operation: automatic; short recoil
Locking system: rising block engaging top of bolt
Length: 1,121 mm (44.1 in)
Weight: 12.9 kg (28.4 lb)
Barrel: 716 mm (28.2 in), four grooves, right-hand twist
Mount: tripod, 3.5 kg (7.7 lb)
Feed system: 250-round fabric belt, or 200-round metal-link belt
Muzzle velocity: 860 m/sec (2,820 ft/sec) with standard ball ammunition
Cyclic rate: 550 rds/min

Dreyse MG. 13   Germany

The MG. 13, or 'Dreyse', was the first machine-gun to be introduced to the German army after the First World War.

Known during clandestine development as 'Gerät 13' to disguise its true purpose, this was introduced in 1928 as the work of Simson & Co. of Suhl – the only gunmaker the Allies trusted to produce automatic weapons. However, it had been designed by Rheinmetall, and was being built secretly in the Sömmerda factory where Rheinmetall's predecessor, Rheinische Metallwaaren- & Maschinenfabrik, had built the 'Dreyse' rifles, pistols and machine-guns.

The MG.13 was a minor adaptation of the older Dreyse design, sharing a recoil-operated breech-lock in which a pivoting bar in the receiver (above the trigger/pistol-grip assembly) locked the bolt securely behind the chambered cartridge. The bar was placed under considerable compressive stress at the instant of firing and could not compare with the strength of

the interrupted-screw lock of the MG. 34 or the pivoting rollers of the MG. 42.

The MG. 13 had a bulky square-contoured receiver and a long barrel within a casing pierced with cooling holes. The trigger activated a hammer that struck a long firing-pin running longitudinally through the bolt body. Pressing the upper segment of the trigger, marked 'E' for Einzelfeuer, gave single shots; pressing the lower portion, marked 'D' for Dauerfeuer, allowed fire to continue automatically until pressure was released.

The MG. 13 was very much lighter than the old water-cooled MG. 08, but could not sustain fire as effectively. An overheating barrel could be replaced only after partially dismantling the gun, unlatching the base of the receiver (which was then swung downward), removing the bolt unit, then withdrawing the barrel – possibly red-hot – backward.

An attempt was made to mount the MG. 13 on a Danish Madsen tripod, for assessment as a medium machine-gun, but feed from 25-round box magazines and the unduly complicated barrel-change doomed the experiments to fail. A special twin-drum 75-round Patronentrommel 13 was developed in the mid 1930s, but proved to be heavy and difficult to load, and also hung awkwardly on the left side of the breech.

The MG. 13 was usually mounted on a bipod, the Zweibein 13, which could be fixed either at the muzzle or the rear of the barrel casing ahead of the carrying handle. Most guns were fitted with flash-hiders, and had a tubular metal-frame butt with a shoulder pad. The butt could be swung back along the right side of the receiver to reduce overall length.

Guns could be attached to the Dreifuss 08/15, necessitating a special adaptor or

Kupplungstück, or directly to the Dreifuss 34. Pedestal mounts for use in pillboxes and strong-points were also made.

Once sufficient new guns had been issued, however, most surviving Dreyse-type guns were sold to Spain during the Civil War (1936-9) or to become the Portuguese 'Metralhadora M/938'. However, a few lasted in second-line, training, police and Volkssturm service until May 1945.

MG. 13k. This short-barrel gun was destined for tanks, vehicles and some aircraft prior to the advent of the MG. 34 and MG. 15.

Designation: Maschinengewehr Modell 13 ('MG. 13')
Made by Simson & Co., Suhl (nominally)

Specification: Standard infantry pattern
Data taken from Ian Hogg and
    John Weeks, Military Small Arms of the
    Twentieth Century, seventh edition,
    2000
Calibre: 7.9 mm (0.311 in)
Chambering: 7.9 x 57, rimless
Operation: selective; short recoil
Locking system: tipping strut behind the
    bolt
Length: 1,466 mm (57.8 in)
Weight: 10.9 kg (23.9 lb) with mount
Barrel: 717 mm (29.3 in), four grooves,
right-hand twist
Mount: bipod

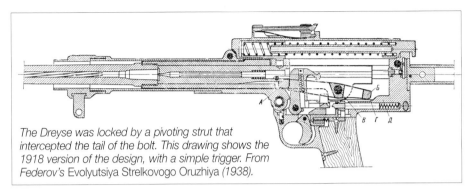

The Dreyse was locked by a pivoting strut that intercepted the tail of the bolt. This drawing shows the 1918 version of the design, with a simple trigger. From Federov's Evolyutsiya Strelkovogo Oruzhiya (1938).

A German gun-crew with an MG. 13, pictured c. 1930. The soldier in the foreground carries a tripod on his back.

Feed system: detachable 25-round box
    magazine or detachable 75-round
    saddle drum
Muzzle velocity: 823 m/sec (2,700 ft/sec)
    with standard ball ammunition
Cyclic rate: 650 rds/min

Rheinmetall MG. 15

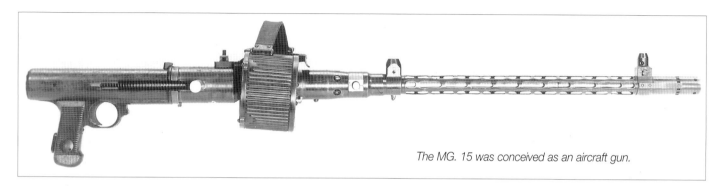

The MG. 15 was conceived as an aircraft gun.

The principal drawbacks of the Solothurn S2-200 (see 'Austria') were shared with the MG. 13: detachable box magazines and a poor barrel-change system. These drawbacks were enough to inhibit use in fire-support roles. Yet the Stange collar-lock mechanism had proved to be efficient, and was perpetuated in the aircraft guns developed by Rheinmetall.

MG. 15 (or 'S6-200'). Developed from the Solothurn S2-200, they had Stange-pattern breech arrangements and locking systems; the MG. 15 also had a wooden butt/spring tube that supported the trigger unit. It is usually encountered with anti-aircraft ring sights, a ball mount and an integral canvas bag to receive ejected cases. The saddle-pattern magazine held 75 rounds, feeding alternately from its two drums. The guns fire from an open bolt.

The MG. 15 needed a suitable bipod for the ground role, though some were adapted for the Norwegian m/29 Browning tripod. The official Luftwaffe ground-role adaptations were created from a kit comprising a purpose-built bipod, a new mainspring-tube and an extension butt similar to that of the MG. 13.

MG. 17 ('T6-200'). This belt-fed gun, intended for fixed installations, could also be adapted to improvised tripod mounts. It fired from a closed bolt to facilitate synchronisation.

MG. 131. An enlargement of the basic system, this 13mm-calibre aircraft gun was rarely encountered on ground mounts. It was made in several versions – 'A' to 'H' – depending on the method of charging, the trigger system, and the direction of feed. The MG131D, for example, was charged pneumatically, had an electro-magnetic trigger, and fed from the left. Two guns in the series ('G' and 'H', with right- and left-side feed respectively) chambered cartridges that were ignited electrically. One or two instances have been reported of MG. 131 emplaced in static defences. These generally prove to have been observers' guns, with pistol grips and special cocking handles. The MG. 131 had a modified Stange collar-lock and an accelerator similar to that of the MG. 13.

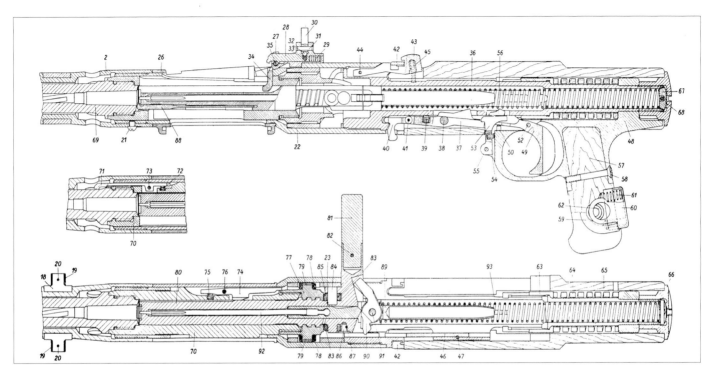

Designation: Maschinengewehr Modell
15 ('MG. 15')
Made by Rheinmetall-Borsig, Sömmerda

Specification: Standard infantry pattern
Data taken from Ian Hogg and
    John Weeks, Military Small Arms of
    the Twentieth Century, seventh edition,
    2000

Calibre: 7.9 mm (0.311 in)
Chambering: 7.9 x 57, rimless
Operation: automatic; short recoil
Locking system: rotating collar
Length: 1,334 mm (52.5 in)
Weight: 12.7 kg (29.0 lb)
Barrel: 595 mm (23.5 in), four grooves,
    right-hand twist
Mount: see text

*Drawings of the MG. 15, from an official
handbook (1941).*

Feed system: detachable 75-round
    saddle drum
Muzzle velocity: 755 m/sec (2,480
    ft/sec) with standard ball ammunition
Cyclic rate: 850 rds/min

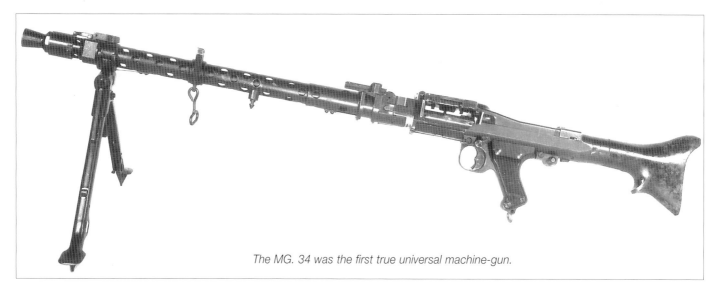

The MG. 34 was the first true universal machine-gun.

The failure of the MG. 13 to address the Einheitsmaschinengewehr concept persuaded the Heereswaffenamt to amalgamate the best features of the guns that had been contesting the trials held in the mid 1930s. Formally approved on 24 January 1939, the MG. 34 had been perfected in Sömmerda under the supervision of Louis Stange and Major Dipl.-Ing. Ritter von Weber.

It retained some of the features of the

MG. 13 and the general appearance of the Solothurn S2-200, but the breech-lock combined Stange's interrupted-screw with the cam-and-roller rotation of the Mauser. Unlike the Solothurn bolt, which moves straight back, the MG. 34 bolt rotates. A recoil booster was fitted to the muzzle to increase the cyclic rate and improve reliability.

The MG. 34 was undoubtedly the most impressive gun of its day, as the

MG-Gerät 34 ('machine-gun system') provided mounts to suit every possible occasion – including the Zweibein 34 (bipod), Dreifuss 34 (tripod), MG-Lafette 34 (buffered quadrupod), Fliegerdrehstütze 36 (pedestal), Zwillingssockel 36 (twin anti-aircraft mount) and the MG-Sockel 41.

Unfortunately, such incredible complexity – the Solothurn-inspired buffered mount alone had more than

An MG. 34, 'somewhere in Russia'. Note the buffered mount that allowed fire to be sustained for long periods.

200 parts – proved to be a terrible production handicap. The MG. 34 could not be made in large enough quantities to satisfy wartime demand, when quantity rather than quality was needed, and the bolt system required particularly careful machining. Combat experience in Russia and North Africa soon showed that key tolerances were much too fine, and that mud, sand or grit often jammed the action.

During the development phase, the Oberkommando der Luftwaffe (OKL) had considered adapting the MG. 34 for airborne use. However, the weight of the gun, and Land Service-inspired features such as the selective-fire trigger and readily exchangeable barrel, prevented a satisfactory transformation. The OKL subsequently purchased the Rheinmetall-developed MG. 15 and, when this was found wanting, then turned to the Mauser MG. 81.

The MG. 34 machine-guns was easily adaptable for tank and vehicle use. An armoured barrel jacket, solid for two-thirds of its length, replaced the standard pierced-sheet pattern in most vehicle roles. The butt, bipod-retaining stud and anti-aircraft sights could be removed to allow the guns to be clamped in special vehicle mounts. However, spare-parts kits comprising a butt, a bipod and a special clamp-mount for the anti-aircraft sight were carried aboard most vehicles to enable the guns to be dismounted for field service.

The standard MG. 34 could feed from a belt (Patronengurt 34) or a detachable 75-round saddle drum (Patronentrommel 34). Cyclic rate was reckoned to be about 800–900 rds/min, depending on the individual gun and the feed system: friction and weight slowed the belt-feed rate compared with spring-feed from the drum. Barrel life, originally about 6,000 rounds, was greatly prolonged by chrome-plating the bore and chamber during the war.

From September 1939 until the end of the war, 345,109 guns were accepted by the HWaA, peak production occurring in 1941 with an additional surge in 1944. Guns were also supplied to Portugal, where they served into the 1970s as 'Metralhadora Mo. 944', while production continued in the Brno factory to equip the post-war Czechoslovakian army.

MG. 34S. After experience in Poland and France, the HWaA requested an increase in the fire-rate as detailed studies had shown – at least in the MG.

34 – that dispersion in short bursts could be reduced. The experimental MG. 34S subsequently achieved cyclic rates as high as 1,650 rds/min, but could not sustain such a hammering for more than a few hundred rounds even though the lock had been modified, an improved recoil booster had been fitted, and the recoil buffer had been greatly strengthened. The MG. 34S was 1,120 mm overall and had a 560 mm barrel.

MG. 34/41. This arose from the failure of the MG. 34S, 1707 guns being despatched to the Eastern Front shortly after the invasion of the Soviet Union. To simplify manufacture and increase the cyclic rate to about 1,250 rds/min, virtually every part of the original gun had been redesigned: the bolt had lugs instead of an interrupted-thread, the feed arrangements were refined, and the trigger was reduced to fully-automatic operation only. However, as the prototype MG. 42 was performing well, the otherwise promising 34/41 was abandoned in January 1943 and the standard MG. 34 remained in production until the end of the war.

Designation: Maschinengewehr Modell 34 ('MG. 34')
Made by Gustloff-Werke, Suhl (formerly Simson & Co.); Maget, Berlin; Mauser-Werke AG, Berlin-Borsigwalde; Steyr-Daimler-Puch AG, Steyr/Oberdonau; and Waffenwerke Brünn AG, Brno.

Specification: Standard infantry pattern
Data taken from Ian Hogg and John Weeks, Military Small Arms of the Twentieth Century, seventh edition, 2000
Calibre: 7.9 mm (0.311 in)
Chambering: 7.9 x 57, rimless
Operation selective; short recoil
Locking system: rotating bolt
Length: 1,219 mm (48.0 in)
Weight: 12.1 kg (26.6 lb) with mount
Barrel: 627 mm (24.8 in), four grooves, right-hand twist
Mount: bipod
Feed system: 50-round belt or detachable 75-round saddle drum
Muzzle velocity: 755 m/sec (2,480 ft/sec) with standard sS ball ammunition
Cyclic rate: 800–900 rds/min

Knorr-Bremse

Germany

The Knorr-Bremse was an interesting, but short-lived design.

Knorr-Bremse of Berlin, an automotive brake-manufacturing company with no previous experience of small-arms production, acquired the rights to a German-financed light machine gun designed in Sweden by Lauf & Przikalla and patented in 1933–4. Prototypes of the 6.5 mm LH/33 had been unsuccessfully offered to Scandinavian governments, and improved 7.9 mm-calibre LH/35 and LH/36 variants were hawked around Germany once Lauf's patents had been assigned to Knorr-Bremse.

The LH/36 was a very distinctive lightweight weapon, with a notable gap between the detachable barrel and the gas port/piston-tube assembly above it. A prominent combination carrying/barrel-changing handle hung down below the feed aperture, into which a detachable 20-round box magazine could be inserted. The bipod collar surrounded the gas tube, which sensibly allowed the barrel to be replaced while the gun remained upright.

The Knorr-Bremse guns were purchased in small quantities by the Waffen-SS, only to be speedily replaced by ZB vz. 26 and vz. 30 light machine-guns after the occupation of Czechoslovakia. Surviving Knorr-Bremse guns were apparently shipped to Finland and expended during the Winter War; a few others had been sold to Sweden, where they served briefly as the 'M40'. Not much was wrong with the basic design but, as the manufacturer had no experience of gunmaking or the demands of military service, some of the components were

simply not robust enough. The butt was prone to working loose during sustained fire and the bolt could run forward and fire the gun if the safety catch was not set properly.

Designation: Maschinengewehr Knorr-Bremse Modell 35
Made by Knorr-Bremse AG, Berlin-Lichtenburg

Specification: Standard infantry pattern
Data taken from Ian Hogg and John Weeks, Military Small Arms of the Twentieth Century, seventh edition, 2000
Calibre: 7.9 mm (0.311 in)
Chambering: 7.9 x 57, rimless
Operation: selective; gas
Locking system: rotating bolt?
Length: 1,308 mm (51.5 in)
Weight: 10.0 kg (22.0 lb) with mount, but without magazine
Barrel: 692 mm (27.3 in), four grooves, right-hand twist
Mount: bipod
Feed system: detachable box magazine, 20 rounds
Muzzle velocity: 792 m/sec (2,600 ft/sec) with standard sS ball ammunition
Cyclic rate: 490 rds/min

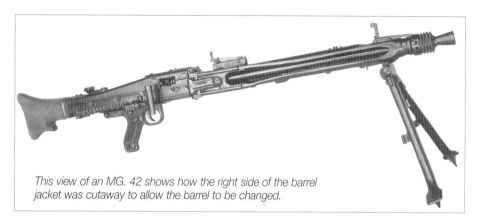

This view of an MG. 42 shows how the right side of the barrel jacket was cutaway to allow the barrel to be changed.

Almost as soon as the MG. 34 had entered production, the OKH began a search for a gun that offered the same performance but was easier to make and less demanding of raw material. However, though metal-stamping would be essential to lift production to the levels that were being demanded, the appropriate technology was still in its infancy.

While these problems were investigated, a draft specification was sent to three leading manufacturers in February 1937. Only one company had experience of weapons design, the others being production specialists. Eventually, Rheinmetall-Borsig A.G. and Stübgen

A.G. of Erfurt submitted gas-operated designs, and Grossfuss Metall- & Lackierwarenfabrik of Döbeln proposed the recoil-operated Grüner system. Grossfuss then built a prototype that convinced the Heereswaffenamt of the merits in its roller-locking system.

The experimental guns had all been completed by April 1938, when trials revealed the unacceptability of the Grossfuss barrel-change. However, as the Rheinmetall and Stübgen designs had failed the tests, an improved Grossfuss gun was requested. Incorporating a one-piece receiver and a better barrel-changing system, this gun performed

much more satisfactorily than its predecessor. Fifty 'MG. 39' were tested at the Döberitz infantry school, and the MG. 39/41, the final pre-production pattern, successfully passed its final field trials in the autumn of 1941. The MG. 42 was approved for mass-production in the summer of 1942, but only 17,250 had been made by the end of the year. By the end of the Second World War, however, more than 400,000 had been made.

Though Grüner had retained the basic MG. 34 concept, the standard metal-link ammunition belt and the multiplicity of mounts, the MG. 42 was far easier to make than its predecessor. In 1944, the cost of an MG. 42 was estimated as 250 Reichsmarks compared with 312 for an MG. 34. Many dimensional tolerances were much wider than had previously been deemed acceptable by the procuring agencies, and the wholesale use of stampings, pressing and welding was viewed with horror by the gunmaking fraternity.

By comparison with the pre-war MG. 34, which displayed excellent surface finish and tightly fitting parts, the MG. 42 was very crude. But it soon proved to be extremely sturdy, despite a stupendous

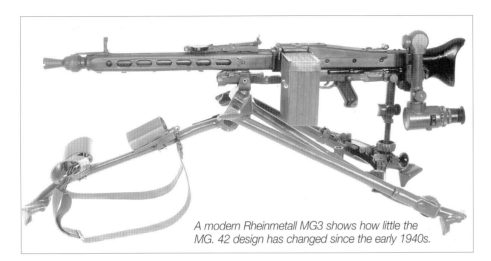

A modern Rheinmetall MG3 shows how little the MG. 42 design has changed since the early 1940s.

rate of fire, and had an exceptionally simple barrel-change system.

Though there are few important variants of the MG. 42, many changes were made during the war to simplify production. The butt, which had originally been of wood, became a synthetic injection moulding; the bipod was greatly simplified; the original straight charging handle was replaced with a toggle-grip lever to ease the cocking effort; and the dimensions of the barrel/barrel bush assembly were so substantially changed that interchangeability could not be guaranteed.

Usually mounted on its simple bipod, the Zweibein 42, the MG. 42 could be transferred to sophisticated buffered quadrupods – the MG.-Lafette 42 and 43 – utilising the standard MG. Z. 34 or MG. Z. 40 optical sights. Mount-types multiplied as the war progressed: not only could the MG. 42 be adapted to fit the standard MG. 34 tripods (Dreifuss 34 and 40) but several differing pedestal, vehicle and anti-aircraft mounts were also in service by 1945.

The unusually high fire-rate gained the nickname Hitlersäge ('Hitler's Saw'), but was undesirable in a lightweight ground gun. The guns consumed huge quantities of ammunition, often to little effect, and even the buffered mounts could vibrate during firing. It was not uncommon to see the German gunners weighting them with sandbags to prevent excessive dispersion of fire. The rapid operating cycle also placed emphasis on the availability of good-quality ammunition, which was not always possible in 1944–5.

Designation: Maschinengewehr Modell 42 ('MG. 42')
Made by Grossfuss, Döbeln; Gustloff-Werke, Suhl; Maget, Berlin; Mauser-Werke AG, Berlin-Borsigwalde; and Steyr-Daimler-Puch AG, Steyr/Oberdonau.

Specification: Standard infantry pattern
Data taken from Ian Hogg and John Weeks, Military Small Arms of the Twentieth Century, seventh edition, 2000
Calibre: 7.9 mm (0.311 in)
Chambering: 7.9 x 57, rimless
Operation: automatic; short recoil
Locking system: rollers on the bolt engaging the barrel-extension walls
Length: 1,219 mm (48.0 in)
Weight: 11.5 kg (25.5 lb) with bipod
Barrel: 533 mm (21.0 in), four grooves, right-hand twist
Mount: bipod or tripod (see text)
Feed system: metal-link belt, 50 rounds
Muzzle velocity: 755 m/sec (2,480 ft/sec) with standard sS ball ammunition
Cyclic rate: 1,200 rds/min

FIAT-Revelli M1914 Italy

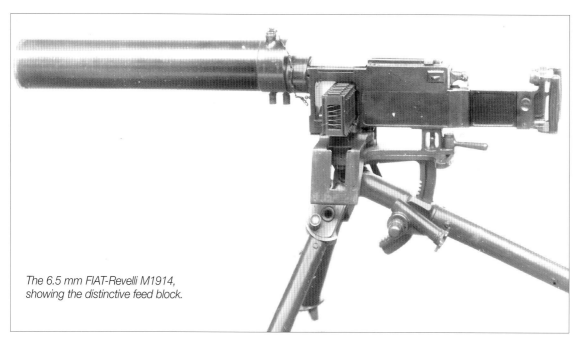

The 6.5 mm FIAT-Revelli M1914, showing the distinctive feed block.

The Italians, after buying a few Maxims early in the twentieth century, spent many years prior to 1914 attempting to perfect the promising machine-gun developed by Giuseppe Perino of Turin arsenal. This recoil-operated gun, considerably lighter than the Maxim, included a bell-crank lever in the breech mechanism to ensure a smooth operating stroke.

Unfortunately, very little had been achieved by October 1914, when, realising the imminence of war with Austria-Hungary, the Italian government ordered 920 Vickers Guns from Britain.

Only 609 of these had been delivered by the end of the month, and there seemed little chance that the remaining 311 would ever be forthcoming. Casting around for an alternative, the authorities gave a second chance to a Revelli design that had been developed as a commercial venture by FIAT. Dating from 1908, this had been extensively tested in June 1913, but, though cheaper than the Maxim, had been rejected after jamming too frequently.

Tests undertaken in November 1914 revealed that the FIAT-Revelli had been improved to a point where it seemed to be acceptable, and it was promptly approved for service. The first guns were delivered in May 1915. However, FIAT had delivered only 500 by the end of 1915 and another contractor – Società Metallurgica Bresciana gia Tempini ('MBT') – was recruited. By the end of the war, MBT had made about 37,500 guns and FIAT had contributed about 10,000, including variants intended for aerial use. Chambered for the standard 6.5 mm rifle cartridge, the M1914 was the principal machine-gun of the Italian army together with the 6.5 mm Colt M1914, being regarded as robust and acceptably reliable as long as it was kept clean. The principal complaint concerned the weight of the gun and coolant, though the cooling system prevented the closed-bolt action 'cooking off' in all but extreme circumstances.

The action was a form of delayed blowback. Though the bolt and the barrel were held together only by a pivoting spring-driven lever in the bottom of the breech, the barrel was allowed to recoil before the bolt was free to overcome the spring-lever and run back to the limit of its travel. The return spring then returned the bolt, thrust a new round into the chamber, and followed the barrel back to battery. The tip of the spring-lever rose into a recess in the underside of the bolt and the gun was ready to fire again.

However, the breech still opened too quickly to prevent case-head separations unless the cartridges were lubricated before entering the chamber. This was achieved with the assistance of an oiler above the breech. The feed was another strange feature. A magazine case, containing 50 rounds in ten rows of five, placed vertically, worked its way through the action from left to right. The guns also had a curious external buffing rod, projecting from the back of the receiver, which reciprocated externally to strike a pad immediately ahead of the back-plate/trigger assembly. A small radial-lever rate regulator on the left rear of the receiver could be set to 'fast' or 'slow'.

M1914/35, or **'M1935'.** FIAT and its subsidiaries had developed a variety of improved Revelli-type machine-guns in the early 1920s, usually with air-cooled detachable barrels and the buffing rod enclosed within the breech. They included small-calibre infantry guns and large-calibre heavy support weapons, customarily fed from tray-type magazines.

The new guns showed that the original 6.5 mm water-cooled guns were too clumsy and underpowered by the standards of the 1930s, so a process of conversion was undertaken by MBT. A new 8 mm-calibre barrel was fitted, with a prominent ring-type carrying handle; the back sight was altered; the water jacket was replaced by a light sheet-steel casing with cooling slots; the quirky magazine gave way to conventional belt feed; and the chamber was fluted to improve extraction. Unfortunately, the M1914/35 still fired from a closed bolt and the barrel proved unable to dissipate heat quickly enough to prevent persistent 'cook-off' problems. The 'improved' guns were actually a retrograde step, even though they served throughout the war.

Designation: Mitraglice FIAT Modello 1914
Made by Fabbrica Italiana Automobili Torino ('FIAT'), Turin, and Società Metallurgica Bresciana gia Tempini ('MBT'), Brescia

Specification: Standard infantry pattern
Data taken from Nicola Pignato, Armi della Fanteria Italiana nella Seconda Guerra Mondiale, 1971
Calibre: 6.5 mm (0.256 in)
Chambering: 6.5 x 52, rimmed
Operation: automatic; delayed blowback
Locking system: none (see text)
Length: 1,250 mm (49.2 in) without flash-hider
Weight: 17.08 kg (37.7 lb) without coolant
Barrel: 645 mm (25.4 in), four grooves, right-hand twist
Mount: tripod
Feed system: compartmented metal carrier, 50 rounds
Muzzle velocity: 680 m/sec (2,230 ft/sec) with standard ball ammunition
Cyclic rate: 300 or 500 rds/min

SIA M1918 Italy

Adopted at the end of the First World War, this was another unsatisfactory design. Credited to Giovanni Agnelli, it was another form of delayed blowback. Unlike the FIAT, however, the SIA had a fixed barrel. The delay was provided – in theory, if not necessarily in practice – by a lug on the firing pin that acted on a cam-surface to rotate the bolt laterally as the action closed. In the original design, a separate hammer then struck the firing pin forward to strike the primer of the chambered round. In the production version, the firing pin, released by a sear on the top rear of the receiver, simply struck the primer a fraction of a second after completing the bolt-rotating stroke.

The SIA had spade grips and a trigger lever on the back plate, an exceptionally slender receiver, and a barrel with cooling fins for most of its length. The feed was a skeletal box magazine on top of the action, which allowed dirt, dust, sand and grit into the action. Like most blowback designs, the breech opened very quickly even though an element of delay was included. Consequently, Agnelli developed a fluted chamber to ease extraction problems, one of the first (if not the first) inventor to use a feature that has since become commonplace.

Though the guns were used for a few years, in both ground and aerial roles, they were never entirely satisfactory and had been discarded by the 1930s. A few survivors, however, reappeared during the Second World War.

Designation: Mitraglice SIA Modello 1918
Made by Società Italiana Ansaldo Armstrong & Co., Rome and Turin

Specification: Standard aircraft observer's pattern
Data taken from Ian Hogg and John Weeks, Military Small Arms of the Twentieth Century, seventh edition, 2000; * indicates approximate figures
Calibre: 6.5 mm (0.256 in)
Chambering: 6.5 x 52, rimmed
Operation: automatic; delayed blowback
Locking system: none (see text)
Length: 1,113 mm (43.8 in)* with spade grips and flash-hider
Weight: 10.2 kg (22.5 lb)*
Barrel: 635 mm (25.0 in),* four grooves, right-hand twist
Mount: ring or pillar
Feed system: detachable box magazine, 30 rounds
Muzzle velocity: 680 m/sec (2,230 ft/sec) with standard ball ammunition
Cyclic rate: 500 rds/min?

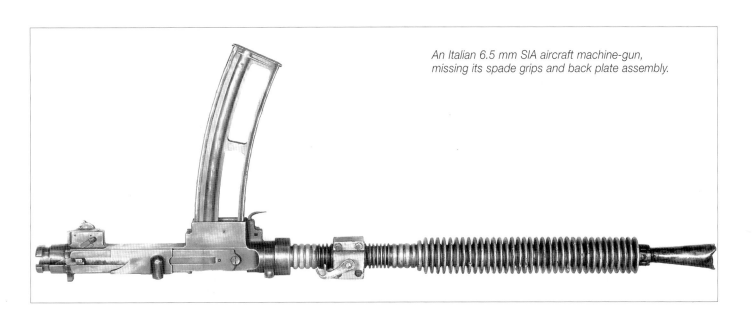

An Italian 6.5 mm SIA aircraft machine-gun, missing its spade grips and back plate assembly.

Breda M1930 Italy

The M1930 Breda light machine-gun, among the most complicated designs in its class.

Developed in the early 1920s, this was another extraordinary design that was full of strange features. These included the absence of a breech lock, forcing the designers to include a lubricating system to ensure that case-head separations were kept to a minimum, and a magazine case that was hinged on the front right side of the feed aperture. The magazine was designed to swing forward, allowing the firer to fill it with rounds stripped from special 20-round chargers, six being supplied with each gun. The Breda also has a detachable barrel with cooling fins, but the absence of a carrying handle makes the gun – which is awkward and ungainly – needlessly difficult to transport.

When the Breda fires, gas pressure through the base of the cartridge forces the barrel, a barrel lock and the bolt to recoil together for about 10 mm. This movement is enough to rotate the barrel-lock, releasing the bolt to run back alone. However, the action is a form of delayed blowback and lacks adequate primary extraction. Consequently, the cartridges are oiled by a cam-operated pump in the top of the receiver as they move from the magazine to the chamber.

The earliest guns, known as 'M1924', had spade grips and were mounted on tripods. Experience showed that they were not particularly effective in heavy-support roles, and subsequent versions were intended primarily as light machine-guns (Mitragliatrici leggere). The M1930 was reclassified in 1935 as a 'machine rifle' (Fucile mitragliatori), which was a better indication of its capabilities. The bipod-mounted Tipo 5C and M1929, which served as the prototypes for the M1930, had sharply raked pistol grips and shoulder stocks.

The M1930 presents a distinctive appearance, with an unusually slender tubular receiver and a trigger aperture that slants noticeably upward ahead of the pistol grip. The pistol grip is closer to vertical than those of the 5C and M1929. The skeletal ladder-type back sight is graduated to 1,500 m, and the front sight is mounted on the tip of the barrel-support cradle. The rear half of the barrel has prominent cooling fins, and a 'T'-bar handle. The magazine lies on the right side of the breech, which means that the gun ejects disconcertingly across the firer, and the butt has a folding shoulder plate. A monopod can also be found, and a few guns were issued with tripods.

The strangest thing about the M1930 was that, despite a multiplicity of curious features and almost unbelievable complexity, it worked surprisingly well. The feed lips were machined in the breech – instead of relying on comparatively flimsy box magazines – and the gun had a reputation for reliable performance as long as the magazine case was undamaged. The Italian army had extensive experience of fighting in sub-Saharan Africa, and even sand does not seem to have affected the Breda unduly. More than 28,000 guns were on hand in August 1939, and work continued throughout the war; 150 were even supplied to the German forces in Italy in May 1944.

M1938. This was a post-1939 conversion of the original 6.5 mm-calibre guns, chambering the more effective 7.35 mm M38 cartridge. As the two cartridges shared the same case-head dimensions, only the barrel was changed.

Designation: Fucile mitragliatrici Breda Modello 1930
Made by Società Anonima Ernesto Breda, Brescia

Specification: Standard infantry pattern
Data taken from Nicola Pignato, Armi della Fanteria Italiana nella Seconda Guerra Mondiale, 1971
Calibre: 6.5 mm (0.256 in)
Chambering: 6.5 x 52, rimmed
Operation: automatic; delayed blowback
Locking system: see text
Length: 1,230 mm (48.4 in) with flash-hider
Weight: 11.0 kg (24.3 lb) loaded
Barrel: 520 mm (20.5 in), four grooves, right-hand twist
Mount: bipod
Feed system: integral box magazine, 20 rounds
Muzzle velocity: 620 m/sec (2,035 ft/sec) with standard ball ammunition
Cyclic rate: 450 rds/min

The 8 mm Breda M1937 was the best of the Italian infantry machine-guns, but still required lubricated ammunition to function effectively.

In 1930, Ernesto Breda obtained a licence to produce the 13.2 mm French Hotchkiss machine-gun, offering the 'Breda M1931' for a variety of infantry, vehicle and aircraft-gun roles. The company also acquired the arms-making subsidiary of FIAT, Società Anonima Fabbrica d'Armi di Torino ('SAFAT'), which had been making a range of machine-guns on the basis of the well-tried Revelli action. The M1935 Breda-SAFAT was a short-recoil gun, locked by a tipping block, and had a fluted chamber to ease extraction problems. Used by the Italian air force in 7.7 mm (0.303 in), the rifle-calibre version was also made in 7.92 x 57. A large-calibre version in 12.7 mm (the British 0.5 Vickers round) and 13.2 x 99 (Hotchkiss) was made for air and naval service respectively.

The M1935 was followed by the rifle-calibre M1937, which became the standard infantry machine-gun of the Second World War. Development had started in 1933, extensive field trials had been undertaken in the Brescia area in 1935–6, and the design had been approved for service in June 1937. It was made in quantity until the end of the Second World War, serving until displaced by the MG. 42/59 in the early 1960s.

Unlike previous Italian service weapons, most of which had been blowbacks of some kind, the M1937 was gas-operated and locked by a titling bolt. Yet it failed to solve extraction problems that had plagued its predecessors, and had a lubricator to oil the cartridges as they entered the chamber. The magazine feed was also unusual. This was due to the origins of this particular Breda, which had been conceived as a tank/vehicle gun. Most machine-guns of this type were fitted with cartridge catchers (often simply a hessian bag covering the ejection port) to prevent spent cartridge cases jamming the turret-rotating mechanism or other machinery within the crew compartment.

The M1937 fed from a tray, inserted from the left; as a new cartridge was pushed forward into the chamber, the spent case was replaced in the tray. When the last round had been fired, the tray could be lifted out of the right side of the gun. Unlike most machine-guns, the M1937 had no need of an ejector.

The M1937 – which also served in Portugal as the 'M1938' – was a sturdy gun, chambered for the 8 x 59 M1935 cartridge and sighted to 3,000 m. It had a deep square-sided receiver, spade grips on the back plate, and a plain cylindrical heavyweight barrel capable of sustaining fire for about 400 rounds without overheating. The mount was customarily a simple (but exceptionally robust) tripod.

M1938. Intended for use in tanks and armoured vehicles, this was a variant of the 1937-type machine-gun with a conventional 24-round detachable box magazine above the breech and an ultra-heavy barrel. A pistol grip and conventional trigger lay beneath the rear of the receiver. The M1938 was 898 mm (35.4 in) long, had a 600 mm (23.6 in) barrel and weighed 16.3 kg (35.9 lb) empty. Cyclic rate was raised to about 550–600 rds/min.

Designation: Mitragliatrice Breda Modello 1937
Made by Società Anonima Ernesto Breda, Brescia

Specification: Standard infantry pattern
Data taken from Nicola Pignato, Armi della Fanteria Italiana nella Seconda Guerra Mondiale, 1971
Calibre: 8 mm (0.315 in)
Chambering: 8 x 59, rebated rim
Operation: automatic; gas
Locking system: tipping block
Length: 1,270 mm (50.0 in) with flash-hider
Weight: 19.4 kg (43.4 lb)
Barrel: 760 mm (29.9 in), four grooves, right-hand twist
Mount: tripod, 18.8 kg (41.4 lb)
Feed system: tray, 20 rounds
Muzzle velocity: 800 m/sec (2625 ft/sec) with standard ball ammunition
Cyclic rate: 450 rds/min

A 7.7 mm Japanese Type 92 Hotchkiss.

The first machine-guns issued to the Japanese army were French Hotchkiss Mitrailleuses Mle 97, bought from the manufacturer and issued as the 'Meiji 30th Year Type', but production subsequently began in Japan. The original guns were widely used during the Russo-Japanese War of 1904–5: for example, the three divisions attacking Port Arthur each had 24. Though intended for use in defensive positions, the machine-guns proved particularly valuable for offensive action, towed on sleds and manoeuvred over obstacles by hand. The Japanese learned the value of a machine-gun for overhead and enfilade fire long before most Western armies came to similar conclusions in the trenches of the First World War.

M1905 (Meiji 38th Year Type). War suggested improvements that could be made in the Hotchkiss, resulting in this gun. Made by Koishikawa Zoheisho in Tokyo under licence, the 38th Year Type appeared in 1905. Many features of its predecessor were retained, but the design of the tripod was noticeably different.

M1914 (Taisho 3rd Year Type). Like the earlier Hotchkiss machine-guns, the Taisho 3rd year type was developed to use the standard 6.5 mm 30th year cartridge, shared with the Arisaka infantry rifles and carbines. However, experience soon showed the action of the 3rd Year Type to be unreliable with the full-charge load. Instead of revising the gun to retain standard ammunition, which would have been advisable, the Japanese decided to retain the gun and simply reduce the power of the cartridge to delay the speed at which the breech opened.

The Japanese 6.5 mm round was intended for a manually operated rifle in which the chamber pressure dropped to

virtually nothing before the breech was opened, but the breech of the machine-gun opened so quickly that residual pressure within the cartridge case tended to hold it against the chamber wall. If this happened, the extractor could tear through the case rim or even separate the case head from the neck. The 3rd Year Type was also prone to excessive headspace, which allowed the base of the cartridge case to set back on firing against the bolt face, also promoting case-head separations when the breech opened.

The advent of the special '3rd Year Type' cartridge was an unwanted complication. Lubrication was still needed to ensure that the parallel-sided cases could slide more easily into the chamber and then extract satisfactorily. The addition of an oiling pad, which coated each cartridge before it entered the breech, promoted acceptable extraction without resorting to pre-lubricated ammunition that tended to attract grit

For the 3rd year type machine-gun the original Hotchkiss-type ejector was replaced by a Lewis pattern, which threw the spent cases out over the bolt. Otherwise the action was much like that of the Hotchkiss, with similar gas operation and a displaced bolt-flap lock. Spade grips replaced the pistol grip of the original Japanese Hotchkiss guns and the

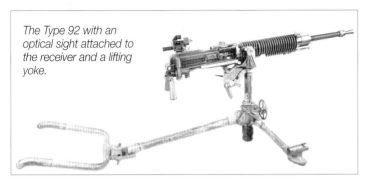
The Type 92 with an optical sight attached to the receiver and a lifting yoke.

barrel was enveloped by large cooling fins.

The distinctive stuttering fire earned the gun the Australian nickname of 'woodpecker' (or 'woodchopper'). Sockets on the legs of the large and heavy tripod allowed the gun to be moved with the assistance of long poles, improving mobility in the type of terrain found in the Far East. A lightened version was developed in the early 1940s, but only a few of the original guns had been converted by the end of the Second World War.

M1932 (Type 92). Little more than a revised and simplified version of the 3rd Year Type, this was chambered for the 7.7 mm semi-rim Type 92 cartridge. The cartridge lubricator was retained to ensure efficient extraction and the original Hotchkiss feed-system was perpetuated, though the strips were pre-loaded and could be linked together to form a continuous belt. The Type 92 had distinctive downward-hinging traverse handles instead of the spade grips of the 3rd

Year Type, and the charging slide lay on the right side of the receiver. Many guns were issued with optical sights, including the 6x Type 93, the 5x Type 94 and 4x Type 96 telescopes, and all made use of a modified 3rd Year Type tripod that could accept a special anti-aircraft adaptor.

The Type 92 could also fire the rimless 7.7 mm Type 99 round, though the Type 99 rifles and light machine-guns would not accept the semi-rim Type 92. Japanese logistics – ammunition supply in particular – were often nightmarish.

Type 93. After two years of negotiation, begun in April 1927, the Kokura army arsenal (trading as the 'Kokura Industrial Company') secured licensing rights to the 1930-type Hotchkiss machine-gun, which was introduced in 1933–4 as the Type 93. This chambered a 13.2 x 99 cartridge and fed from a top-mounted spring-loaded box magazine holding 30 rounds. Originally intended as an anti-aircraft weapon, issued with special sights and mount, it was also used for infantry support and anti-tank warfare.

Type 1. Experience in Manchuria in the late 1930s showed that the Type 92 was too heavy to manhandle easily, so a lighter

version was tested in 1940 and eventually accepted for service as the Type 1. Some of the trial weapons were fitted with a German-type sled mount, reminiscent of the old MG. 08, but the finalised design had a light tripod and a readily detachable barrel inspired by trials with modifications of the Type 99. The Type 1 machine-guns could only chamber the rimless Type 99 round, and not the semi-rim Type 92.

Designation: Kuni shiki jukikanju
Made by Kokura army arsenal

Specification: Standard Type 92
Data taken from George Markham, Japanese Infantry Weapons of World War 2 1976 and (*) from Ian Hogg and John Weeks, Military Small Arms of the Twentieth Century, seventh edition 2000
Calibre: 7.7 mm (0.303 in)
Chambering: 7.7 x 58, semi-rim
Operation: automatic; gas
Locking system: flaps on the bolt engaging the receiver walls
Length: 1,155 mm (45.5 in)
Weight: 27.6 kg (60.8 lb) without mount
Barrel; 698 mm (27.5 in), 4 grooves, left-hand twist*
Mount: tripod
Feed system: metal strip, 30 rounds (can be joined together)
Muzzle velocity: 732 m/sec (2,400 ft/sec) with standard Type 92 ball ammunition*
Cyclic rate: 450 rds/min

Taisho 11th Year Type

Japan

The 6.5 mm Taisho 11th Year Type light machine-gun had a hopper magazine on the left side of the breech.

Observing combat during the First World War, and the introduction of weapons such as the Lewis Gun, persuaded the Japanese to develop a light machine-gun of their own. The Taisho 11th Year Type was adopted in 1922, when the Taisho 3rd Year Type was reclassified as a heavy machine-gun (jukikanju).

The 11th Year Type combined the well-proven Hotchkiss action with an unusual spring-fed hopper magazine, mounted on the left of the receiver and loaded with six 5-round rifle chargers that acted as clips. Single rounds were then stripped into the

chamber each time the bolt returned from the full-recoil position, the process being repeated until the first 5-round charger was expended. The spring-loaded follower plate then ejected the empty charger through the underside of the hopper, and the first round of the second charger was fed into the breech.

The process continued until all six chargers had been emptied, though the hopper could be continuously replenished during lulls in firing. The intention was to use standard rifle chargers, simplifying ammunition supply by eliminating the

Hotchkiss strips. Unfortunately, the hopper was complicated and unreliable, and special reduced-charge ammunition was needed to prevent case-head separations during extraction.

Regulation-issue rifle ammunition could be used in an emergency, but recoil was much more violent and extraction troubles persisted. To make matters worse, the ejector was exposed to the elements on the left rear of the receiver.

Type 89 army aircraft machine-gun, flexible. In the late 1920s, when suitable machine-guns were required by both the

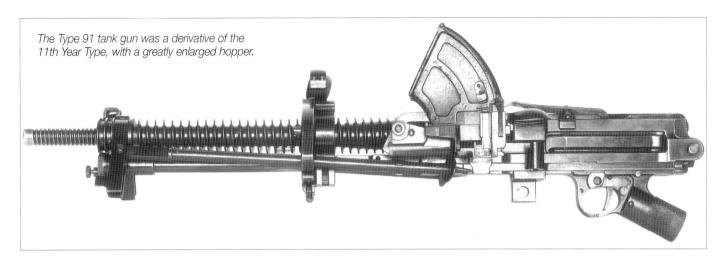

The Type 91 tank gun was a derivative of the 11th Year Type, with a greatly enlarged hopper.

army and navy air forces, this modification of the 11th Year Type weapon was developed. It chambered a new 7.7 mm Type 89 cartridge (a copy of the British 0.303 in rimmed round) to avoid the problems that had arisen in the 11th Year Type with 6.5 mm ammunition, and had a 70-round pan magazine copied from the Lewis. A few Type 89 guns, mounted on rudimentary bipods, were used by ground forces in the closing stages of the Second World War.

Type 91 tank machine-gun. Developed from the 11th Year Type in 1931, this had an enlarged hopper accepting 10 5-round chargers. Most guns also had a large 1.5x telescope sight on the right of the receiver.

Shoulder stocks and bipods were carried aboard tanks and vehicles, allowing the guns to be dismounted if required, and many survivors – displaced by the Type 97 – were pressed into ground service at the end of the war in the Pacific.

Designation: Taisho juichi nenshiki keikikanju
Made by Koishikawa and other state arsenals

Specification: Standard infantry pattern
Data taken from Ian Hogg and John Weeks, Military Small Arms of the Twentieth Century, seventh edition, 2000

Calibre: 6.5 mm (0.256 in)
Chambering: 6.5 x 52, semi-rim
Operation: automatic; gas
Locking system: flaps on the bolt engaging the receiver walls
Length: 1,104 mm (43.5 in)
Weight: 10.2 kg (22.5 lb) with mount
Barrel: 482 mm (19.0 in), four grooves, right-hand twist
Mount: bipod
Feed system: hopper, 30 rounds
Muzzle velocity: 701 m/sec (2,300 ft/sec) with standard ball ammunition
Cyclic rate: 500 rds/min

Type 89

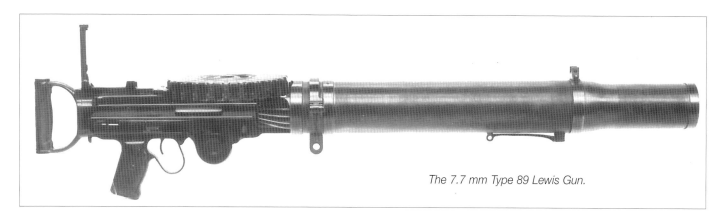

The 7.7 mm Type 89 Lewis Gun.

In 1929 the naval air service adopted the air-cooled Type 89 (naval) aircraft flexible gun, a 7.7 mm Lewis-system machine-gun, which fed from a 97-round two-tier pan magazine – although the standard British 47-round magazine, which accepted the Type 89 (British 0.303 in) rimmed cartridge, could also be used. There was a spade grip instead of a shoulder stock, and the pistol grip had an enlarged trigger guard to give access for a gloved finger. Type 89 naval guns were widely used on small ships and some, fitted on crude bipods, saw land service in the closing stages of the Second World War. A modification was apparently made

in 1932, retaining the two-tier pan magazine and chambered for the 7.7 mm rimmed Type 89 round. It had a barrel jacket and spade grips, and its tripod could easily be adapted for infantry or anti-aircraft use. The mount was capable of a depression of 80° and an elevation of 85°, without removing the gun.

Designation
Made by Yokosuka navy arsenal

Specification: Standard Type 89
Data taken from George Markham,
Japanese Infantry Weapons of World
War 2, 1976

Calibre: 7.7 mm (0.303 in)
Chambering: 0.303 in (7.7 x 56R)
Operation: automatic; gas
Locking system: rotating bolt
Length: 990 mm (39.0 in)
Weight: 11.0 kg (24.3 lb)
Barrel: 610 mm (24.0 in), four grooves, right-hand twist
Mount: see text
Feed system: detachable pan, 47 rounds
Muzzle velocity: 685 m/sec (2,245 ft/sec) with standard Type 89 ball ammunition
Cyclic rate: 600 rds/min

Type 96 and 99 Japan

The 7.7 mm Type 99 of 1939 was the first Japanese light machine-gun to combine a detachable box magazine with a cartridge offering reasonable power.

By 1936, designs were ready for a much-needed successor to the light 11th year type. The resulting Type 96 was a modification of the ubiquitous Hotchkiss gas-operation system, but the old hopper magazine was replaced by a spring-feed box magazine on top of the receiver. A quick-change barrel was also developed. But the 11th year type's extraction troubles persisted largely because Type 96 was still chambered for the 6.5 mm cartridge. The lubricator was built into the magazines rather than the gun mechanism, removing the need for a separate reservoir in the receiver.

The Type 96 had a distinctive combined shoulder stock and pistol grip, with a carrying handle above the barrel in front of the magazine. The standard 30th year type bayonet could be fitted around the gas cylinder but, once the barrels were fitted with flash-hiders, the protrusion of the bayonet past the muzzle was minimal; the guns themselves, however, were sufficiently light to be used for the old French practice of 'assault at the walk'.

Type 99. Prompted by experience in Manchuria, with its extremes of temperature, experiments began in 1937 to develop a new light gun without a lubricator. The Type 99 resembled the Type 96 externally, though there were differences in the machining of the receiver and in the design of the barrel latch. Headspace was adjustable. The new magazine was not so sharply curved as its predecessor and a monopod could be fitted beneath the butt. The Type 99 had a distinctive flash-hider, but similar fittings will be encountered on the Type 96. Guns could also be fitted with a 2.5x Type 96 telescope sight and an armour-plate shield for use in defensive positions.

Type 1 Model 1. A paratrooper's version of the Type 99 developed by Nagoya army arsenal, this had a quick-detachable barrel. Made only in small numbers, it had a characteristic hollow steel pistol grip that could be folded forward to protect the trigger and trigger guard. The magazine and the barrel could be separated from the receiver, to fit into a paratrooper's leg pouch, but these subassemblies were still heavy and cumbersome.

Designation: Kuku shiki keikikanju
Made by Kokura and Nagoya army
 arsenals and other state-run factories

Specification: Standard Type 99
Data taken from Ian Hogg &
 John Weeks, Military Small Arms of the
 Twentieth Century, seventh edition 2000
Calibre: 7.7 mm (0.303 in)
Chambering: 7.7 x 58, rimless
Operation: automatic; gas
Locking system: flaps on the bolt
 engaging the receiver walls
Length: 1,181 mm (46.5 in)
Weight: 10.4 kg (23.0 lb) with mount
Barrel: 545 mm (21.5 in), four grooves,
 right-hand twist
Mount: bipod
Feed system: detachable box magazine,
 30 rounds
Muzzle velocity: 715 m/sec (2,350 ft/sec)
 with standard Type 99 ball ammunition
Cyclic rate: 800 rds/min

Type 97 — Japan

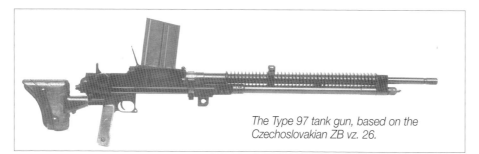

The Type 97 tank gun, based on the Czechoslovakian ZB vz. 26.

Advances in tank machine-gun design made the Type 91 obsolete and the Type 97 was introduced. Copied from the ZB vz. 26, the Japanese version was slightly modified, but the basic system – gas-operated and locked by camming the breechblock into the top of the receiver remained unaltered. Issued with the 1.5x Type 91 telescope sight and an armoured barrel cover, Type 97 worked equally well with the 7.7 mm semi-rim Type 92 or 7.7 mm rimless Type 99 ammunition, and the cartridge lubricator was eliminated as a result of improved design.

Type 100 army aircraft machine-guns. The army air service adopted a strange double-barrelled flexible machine-gun, the Type 100, which promised a greater volume of fire than the regular single barrel guns. The two breech mechanisms, one for each

barrel, were contained in a single receiver block, so two guns could be mounted in the space occupied by one conventional gun.

The action was adapted from the Type 97 tank weapons, but the feed was a saddle-drum similar to that of the Type 98 (the Rheinmetall-made MG. 15). Each side of the magazine held 50 rounds and separate feed springs ensured that if one barrel jammed the other kept firing. The Type 100 had double trigger units, but pressure on either trigger would fire both barrels.

Type 1. A variant of the Type 100, this had a shoulder rest made of wood and canvas, attached to the receiver by a steel frame.

Designation: Kunana shiki shasai kikanju
Made by Japanese state ordnance factories

Specification: Standard Type 97
Data taken from George Markham, Japanese Infantry Weapons of World War 2, 1976
Calibre: 7.7 mm (0.303 in)
Chambering: 7.7 x 58, semi-rim
Operation: automatic; gas
Locking system: tilting block engaging the roof of the receiver
Length: 1,180 mm (46.5 in)
Weight: 11.1 kg (24.5 lb)
Barrel: 712 mm (28.0 in), four grooves, right-hand twist
Mount: see text
Feed system: detachable box, 30 rounds
Muzzle velocity: 700 m/sec (2,295 ft/sec) with standard Type 92 ball ammunition
Cyclic rate: 500 rds/min

The Japanese Type 1 twin-barrelled aircraft machine-gun of 1941.

Maxim M1905 and M1910 ('PM')   Russia

The Russian 7.62 x 54R M1910 Maxim, on a Sokolov mount. Note the two additional legs that can be used to raise the mount off the ground.

The first Maxims to be tested in Russian dated from 1887, obtained through the agencies of the Maxim Machine Gun Company, but performed poorly. Problems arose with the standard 10.6 mm rimmed rifle cartridge and not until 1895 – after improvements had been made, and a 7.62 mm cartridge had been adopted – was the 'Russian Maxim' adopted as a regulation weapon. The earliest guns were apparently supplied from Britain, but assembly then began in the Tula ordnance factory using British-made parts.

The guns served with distinction during the Russo-Japanese War, but protracted combat showed that they still had flaws. A new version was adopted in 1905, when Tula began to make guns in their entirety, and an improved version was approved in 1910. The 1905-type guns had bronze water jackets and bronze hand grips, and weighed about 28.25 kg (62.3 lb) empty; the perfected 1910 version had a sheet-steel jacket, wooden hand grips, and a weight of only 18.43 kg (40.6 lb). The M1905 was sighted to 2000 paces for the M1891 cartridge, but the M1910 was sighted to 3,200 paces for the M1908 or 'Type L' ball round. The alterations have been credited in the Soviet Press to Tretyakov and Pastukhov of the Tula factory staff.

The original Maxims were issued on a massive tripod, which Fedorov calls the 'Kolesniy lafet trenoga'; the later guns were fitted on to a complicated (but much lighter) wheeled mount credited to Sokolov, which had a 'U'-shape trail and two additional legs that could serve as a tripod. The mount also had a wheeled axle, and, in the original pattern at least, a small third wheel at the rear of the trail.

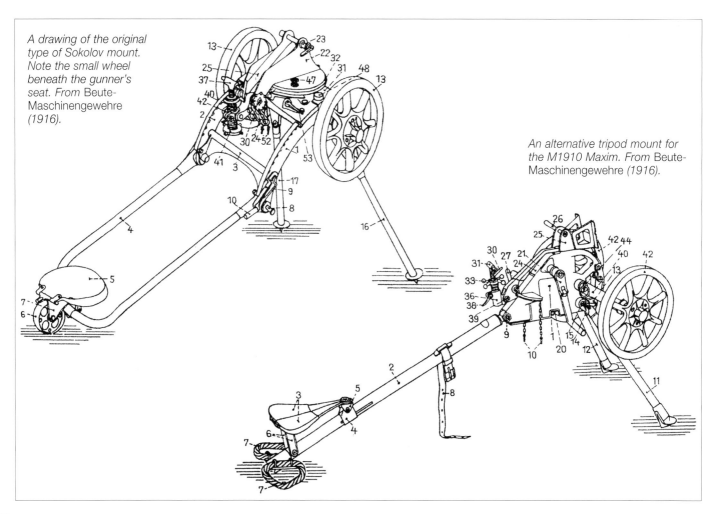

A drawing of the original type of Sokolov mount. Note the small wheel beneath the gunner's seat. From Beute-Maschinengewehre (1916).

An alternative tripod mount for the M1910 Maxim. From Beute-Maschinengewehre (1916).

The guns made during the First World War followed the pre-1914 pattern, but often had ribbed barrel jackets. Like all Maxims, they were recoil-operated, belt-fed and water-cooled, additional thrust on the 1910 version being imparted to the recoiling breech block by trapping gases at the muzzle. This raised the cyclic rate to about 450 rds/min. The wartime 'new pattern' Sokolov mount abandoned the additional legs and the trail-wheel, and a 'Universal' tripod was introduced in 1915. This had a pole trail, though it also had a wheeled axle to facilitate transport. Both mounts were sometimes fitted with a 9 kg (20 lb) steel shield to protect the firer.

The sights comprised a folding-bar back sight, fitted with a 'peep' or aperture, and a barleycorn front sight offset to the left to avoid the water inlets. A bracket for an optical sight was customarily fixed to the left side of the receiver of the M1910, but absent from the M1905.

Designation: Pulemet Maxima. Obrazets 1905 goda
Made by Tula small-arms factory

Specification: Standard M1905
Data taken from V. G. Fedorov, Evolyutsiya Strelkovogo Oruzhiya – II. Razvitie avtomaticheskogo oruzhiya , 1938
Calibre: 7.62 mm (0.300 in)
Chambering: 7.62 x 54, rimmed
Operation: automatic; short recoil
Locking system: toggle lock, breaking downward
Length: 1,100 mm (43.3 in)
Weight: of gun 28.3 kg (62.3 lb) with coolant
Barrel: 720 mm (28.3 in), four grooves, right-hand twist
Mount: wheeled tripod, 195.5 kg (431lb) with shield
Feed system: fabric belt, 100 or 250 rounds
Muzzle velocity: 640 m/sec (2,100 ft/sec) with standard M1891 ball ammunition
Cyclic rate: 300 rds/min

These German machine-gunners are pictured testing Russian M1910 Maxims captured on the Eastern Front.

A Turkish MG. 08, made by DWM in 1915, mounted on the 1916-pattern German tripod.

Turkey was an avid purchaser of German weapons, a relationship that stretched back to the 1880s. Huge quantities of Mauser magazine rifles had been acquired from 1887 onward, and, although the first deliveries of Maxims had come from Britain, it was only natural that the Turks should turn to the Germans for large-scale supplies.

The most significant of the purchases was the M1909 'export' Maxim made by Deutsche Waffen- & Munitionsfabriken, which was essentially the regulation MG. 08 mounted on a tripod instead of a sledge. The back sight was also different, though the gun chambered the 7.9 x 57 mm cartridge instead of the 7.65 mm pattern associated with many of the Turkish Mauser rifles.

The Maxims served throughout the First World War, alongside a number of genuine wartime MG. 08 and Bergmann water-cooled guns that had been sent to Turkey once German industry had been able to deliver sufficient Maxims.

Some of the Turkish guns were fitted to old British tripods, captured during the Gallipoli campaign, and some of the German tripods acquired anti-aircraft adaptors in the period between the wars. The Turkish guns customarily bear the marks of the manufacturer (usually DWM), but can be dated between 1910 and 1918. Only the pre-war contract guns bore Turkish

Another Turkish MG. 08, made by DWM in 1918, mounted on a captured British Mark I Maxim/Vickers tripod.

markings; those supplied during the First World War invariably displayed standard German makers', proof and inspectors' marks.

Colt M1895 USA

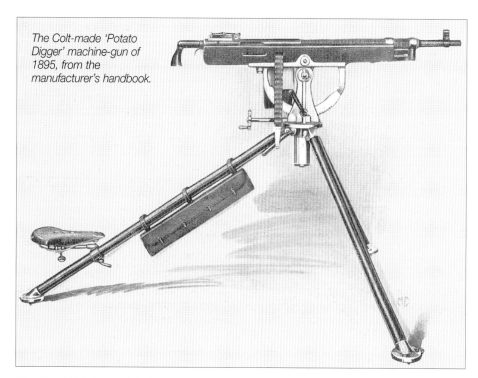

The Colt-made 'Potato Digger' machine-gun of 1895, from the manufacturer's handbook.

American Wars had shown the potential of the machine-gun, the US Army tested a .30-calibre British-pattern Maxim (the disliked wheeled mount was replaced by a tripod soon after submission), the M1895 Colt-Browning and a .30-calibre strip-feed Hotchkiss. The water-cooled Maxim was preferred to the quirky Hotchkiss and the otherwise efficient Colt, as it could deliver a greater volume of sustained fire than either of its air-cooled rivals.

A licence to make the Maxim in the USA was negotiated, but the army simply brought its first 282 'Maxim Automatic Machine Guns, Caliber .30, Model of 1904' from Vickers, Sons & Maxim in Britain. Rechambered for the .30 M1906 cartridge, the guns proved to be sturdy and dependable.

The basis of the gas-operated .30-calibre Colt Automatic Machine Gun had been patented by John Browning in 1889. The radial operating lever pivoted downward when gas was bled from the muzzle and forced the bolt back to complete the extraction/reloading cycle. This gave a smooth action, but required a space of at least eight inches beneath the gun to prevent the actuating lever burying itself in the ground. The

The first USA Army trial of a Maxim 'Automatic Machine Gun' occurred in 1890, when the testing board was sufficiently impressed to recommend that additional guns be acquired for troop trials. However, money was short and the army authorities were well satisfied with the hundreds of service Gatlings. Nothing further happened until in 1900, after the experience of the Spanish-

nickname 'Potato Digger' shows how aware its operators were of this feature.

The US Navy purchased about 210 of 'Mark 1' Colts for shipboard use – half in 0.236, the remainder in 30–40 Krag – and others were acquired for the US Marine Corps. Though never standardised, the army purchased at least 100 'M1895' Colts in 30-40; the militia took approximately 75. Most survivors were converted to the 0.30 M1906 cartridge in 1906–12. These were known in the Navy as 'Mark 1 Model 1', and in the army as 'M1895 converted'. Many were still on the inventory when the US forces entered the First World War in 1917.

M1915. Also known as the 'Mark III' (or 'M1917 to the US Army), this was a minor variant of the original Colt developed by the Canadian ordnance authorities. It had cooling fins on the barrel and a lightened tripod, but the most obvious feature was the cable-type retractor on the left side of the breech with a drum on the front left side of the gas-port block. This ensured that the action could be charged from the rear. Some of the guns were supplied to the Russians at the beginning of the First World War, but production was soon licensed to the Marlin Arms Company (renamed 'Marlin-Rockwell' in 1916). The Canadian Army also successfully used Colts on the Western Front until they were retired in favour of the Vickers. About 4,800 improved Colts were purchased by the US authorities during the First World War, 1,500 of which went to the US Navy that already had 400 of original M1895 Colt-made guns converted for the 0.30 M1906 cartridge.

M1916. At the request of the US Navy, Marlin replaced the original radial actuating lever with a straight-line piston in a successful attempt to provide a gun that could work with a synchroniser. Though most of the parts remained interchangeable with the M1915, changes were required to slow the opening of the breech, minimise case-head separations and reduce the number of extractors broken by the violence of the revised action.

M1917 (July 1917). No sooner had the aircraft gun been perfected than a hydro-pneumatic synchroniser replaced the original mechanical pattern. This forced changes to made in the design of the gun, and the M1917 was the result. Marlin made 13,235 of them.

M1918 (June 1918). Converted from the 1917-pattern aircraft gun, this tank gun could be distinguished by a large aluminium radiator and a pistol grip. Production amounted to 428 by the end of the war, though sufficient parts were on hand in November 1918 to allow 2,583 more machine-guns to be assembled in 1919.

Designation: US Machine Gun, Caliber 0.30-inch, Model of 1918 ('M1918 tank gun')
Made by the Marlin-Rockwell Corporation, New Haven, Connecticut, USA

Specification: Standard pattern
Data taken from Ian Hogg and John Weeks, Military Small Arms of the Twentieth Century, seventh edition, 2000
Calibre: 7.62 mm (0.300 in)
Chambering: 0.30 M1906 ('30-06'), rimmed
Operation: automatic; gas
Locking system: tipping bolt engaging the roof of the receiver
Length: 1,016 mm (40.0 in)
Weight: 10.2 kg (22.5 lb)
Barrel: 711 mm (28.0 in), four grooves, right-hand twist
Mount: rigidly on aircraft
Feed system: fabric belt, 250 rounds
Muzzle velocity: 853 m/sec (2,800 ft/sec) with standard ball ammunition
Cyclic rate: 600 rds/min

Benét-Mercié M1909 USA

The only other automatic machine-gun to be adopted in the USA prior to 1914 was the 0.30-calibre Benét-Mercié Machine Rifle, a lightened version of the standard Hotchkiss patterns described in the French section. Interestingly, Francophile Laurence Benét was the son of a former US Army Chief of Ordnance. The Benét-Mercié had been the best of the guns submitted to trials in 1908 – rather surprisingly being preferred to the Madsen – and was officially adopted in 1909. About 1070 guns were subsequently made in Springfield Armory or by Colt: 670 for the army, 400 for the navy and the marines.

The M1909 had a combined shoulder-stock/pistol grip and a bipod, though a butt-monopod and a fragile tripod were also available. The guns acquired a particularly unfortunate reputation after a raid by Pancho Villa on Columbus, New Mexico, where four Benét-Mercié guns were available. Journalists, basing their views on claims that the guns were difficult to load in the dark, assumed that firing lapses were due to jams instead of the absence of targets. Consequently, the M1909 was labelled the 'Daylight Gun' and the unwanted reputation persisted even though investigations revealed that the four guns had fired 20,000 rounds with only an occasional jam. Yet despite its failings, the Benét-Mercié was widely regarded as the only machine-gun necessary for the US Army until the water-cooled Vickers was adopted in 1915.

Designation: US Machine Rifle, Caliber 0.30-inch, Model of 1909
Made by Société Anonyme des anciens établissements Hotchkiss et Cie, Saint-Denis, France, the National Armory, Springfield, Massachusetts, and Colt's Patent Fire Arms Mfg Co., Hartford, Connecticut, USA

Specification: Standard infantry pattern
Data taken from Maj.-Gen. Julian S. Hatcher, Hatcher's Notebook, 1956
Calibre: 7.62 mm (0.300 in)
Chambering: 0.30 M1906 ('30-06'), rimless
Locking system: pivoting struts on the bolt engaging the receiver walls
Length: 1,190 mm (46.9 in)
Weight: 12.5 kg (27.6 lb) with bipod
Barrel: 565 mm (22.2 in), four grooves, left-hand twist
Mount: bipod, with an optional monopod beneath the butt
Feed system: metallic strip, 30 rounds
Muzzle velocity: 853 m/sec (2,800 ft/sec) with standard ball ammunition
Cyclic rate: 500 rds/min

Lewis

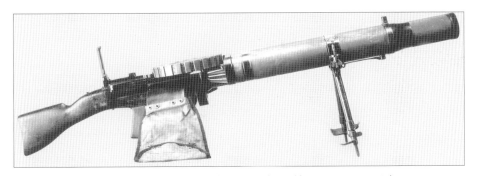

A typical Savage-made 0.30 M1915 Lewis Gun, complete with canvas case catcher.

The first US Army trials guns, made by Savage, chambered the British rimmed 0.303 cartridge. They passed the tests satisfactorily, but the manufacturer was asked to convert the Lewis Gun for the standard rimless 0.30 M1906 cartridge – much powerful than the British round, and notoriously difficult to extract. The first experiments were disastrous, as many parts broke and the guns persistently jammed.

Alterations were subsequently made to lengthen the cam dwell, slowing the action, but the improvements were not enough. Though the 0.30 Lewis worked more efficiently after the modifications had been made, trials in April 1916 still registered 206 jams and 35 broken parts during the 20,000-round endurance trial. The competing Vickers Gun recorded 23 stoppages, no parts breakages, and was promptly approved.

Expecting the Lewis Gun to out-perform a water-cooled medium machine-gun was clearly unreasonable, and its true value remained unappreciated until the war began. The US Army bought only 350 0.303 Savage-Lewis Guns to replace the Benét-Mercié machine rifles along the Mexican border.

When the USA entered the First World War, and machine-guns were in short supply, the Lewis Guns were acquired in larger numbers. However, the US Navy and the Marine Corps did not share the negative opinions of the army, buying 4,204 guns compared with only 2500.

Model 1918. This was a highly successful airborne derivative of the .30 Lewis Gun, with the original 47- or supplementary 97-round pan magazine: 32,231 had been completed by November 1918, followed by about 7,500 in 1919.

Designation: US Light Machine-Gun, Caliber 0.30-inch, Lewis Model of 1915
Made by the Savage Arms Company, Utica, New York State, USA

Specification: Standard pattern
Data taken from Maj.-Gen. Julian S. Hatcher, Hatcher's Notebook, 1956
Calibre: 7.62 mm (0.300 in)
Chambering: 0.30 M1906 ('30-06'), rimmed
Operation: gas; automatic fire only
Locking system: rotating bolt
Length: 1,283 mm (50.5 in)
Weight: 11.8 kg (26.0 lb)
Barrel 666 mm (26.3 in), four grooves, left-hand twist
Mount: bipod
Feed system: pan, 47 rounds
Muzzle velocity: 853 m/sec (2,800 ft/sec) with standard ball ammunition
Cyclic rate: 500 rds/min

The water-cooled M1917A1 Browning machine-gun, among the very best of its type, had an unrivalled reputation for reliability.

This was created by John M. Browning on the basis of patents dating back to 1901. Rejected in 1916, the Browning was tested again in May 1917, under the threat of war, and performed sensationally. By the end of the test period, one of the guns had fired 396,000 rounds, with only a few stoppages, and was still in full working condition.

The Browning was easier and cheaper to make than its Vickers or Hotchkiss rivals, and so it was ordered into mass-production virtually from the testing ground. A 15,000-gun contract was given to Remington, though a 10,000-gun contract due to be given to Colt, charged with producing the master drawings, was delayed until October 1917. Finally, in January 1918, 20,000 were ordered from the New England Westinghouse Company. By the Armistice, about 43,750 guns had been made, but assembly continued into 1919 and finally totalled about 69,000.

Combat experience with the Browning was excellent, and the M1917 rapidly replaced the Vickers Gun in front-line service. Protracted service showed that there was an inherent weakness in the bottom of the receiver, but a reinforcing plate was simply welded on to surviving guns in the 1920s.

M1917A1 (1936). While the air-cooled M1919A4 was being perfected, minor changes had also been made to the standard water-cooled gun, and the M1917A1 was adopted. All the existing M1917 service guns were then updated by Rock Island Arsenal, replacing the old weak receiver bottom-plate with a strengthened pattern, improving the feed lever and the feed cover, and re-calibrating the sights. Colt continued production throughout the Second World War, a steel water jacket replacing the bronze version in 1942 to conserve raw material. By 1945, 53,854 M1917A1 guns had been made.

M1918. An air-cooled transformation of the water-cooled M1917, the M1918 aircraft gun was unsuccessful.

M1918A1. A replacement for the abortive M1918, this had a modified trigger assembly and an improved mounting.

M1919 (aircraft). This purpose-built gun was appreciably more successful that the M1918, though the merits of interchangeability had been lost in the transformation. Production was comparatively small.

M1919 (tank). Developed for use in the Mk VIII tank, this was not standardised until after the Armistice. Distinctive features included a 457 mm (18 in) barrel, a slotted barrel casing, an optical sight and a ball mount. A tube sight and a special small tripod were issued to permit the gun to be dismounted from the tank when required. However, the tank gun was not especially successful and virtually all survivors were converted to M1919A4 standards.

M1919A1 (1931). After protracted trials, the first purpose-built air-cooled ground gun was created from the M1919 tank

The air-cooled M1919A4 Browning.

This M1919A4 Browning is seen in the hands of British troops serving in Korea. Browning-type vehicle guns are still in service in small numbers.

vehicle and dismounted use. The mechanism proved acceptable, but the combination of a new open back sight and the front sight mounted on the barrel casing proved calamitous; by 1941, all surviving 'A2' guns had been converted to A4 standards.

M1919A4. The perfected design had a 610 mm (24 in) barrel, reducing the cyclic rate but improving the action. With the back sight on the cover plate and the front sight on the trunnion block, and a greatly improved tripod, the gun was adopted to replace all the previous Browning air-cooled guns.

M1919A5. A tank-gun derivative of the M1919A4, this had a ball mount and lacked sights.

M1919A6. The final result of tests held in 1942–3 was the standardisation of this 0.30-calibre gun, with a shoulder stock attached to the rear of the receiver and a bipod at the muzzle. This gun was very successful, though its considerable weight, which contributed greatly to its stability in sustained fire, reduced its portability. About 43,479 were made in 1943-6, later examples having permanently mounted tripod adaptors, rotary carrying handles and synthetic furniture.

M2 (March 1931). Though the Browning ground gun had proved outstandingly successful, the tank and aircraft versions had not been so effectual. In 1921–2, therefore, a new purpose-built aircraft gun

pattern. A sight was mounted on the trunnion block at the front of the receiver, a new tube-type back sight lay above the receiver, and the tank-type

ball mount was removed. Unfortunately, the M1919A1 had too many flaws and was soon replaced by the M1919A2, developed by the Cavalry Board for

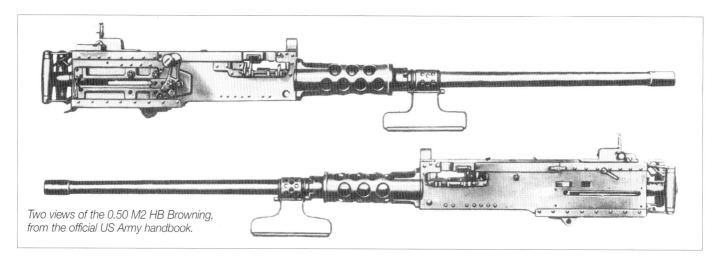

Two views of the 0.50 M2 HB Browning, from the official US Army handbook.

appeared, with convertible feed and good synchronization compatibility achieved by abandoning commonality with the M1917. The new weapon was successfully tested in 1922, but there was so little funding available that the army turned the project over the Colt's Patent Fire Arms Manufacturing Company. Colt was permitted to exploit the project commercially in return for completion of development through to the mass-production stage. Work was completed in 1929 and the '.30 Aircraft Machine Gun, M2' was adopted two years later. However, though nearly 194,000 M2 aircraft guns were made during the Second World War (including 70,000 sent

to Britain under Lend-Lease), the 0.50 M2 was preferred in the USAF.

Designation: US Machine Gun, Caliber 0.30-inch, Browning Model of 1917
Made by the Remington Arms Company, Bridgeport, Connecticut; Colt's Patent Fire Arms Manufacturing Company, Hartford, Connecticut; and the New England Westinghouse Company, Bridgeport, Connecticut, USA.

Specification: Standard M1917A1
Data taken from Ian Hogg and
John Weeks, Military Small Arms of the Twentieth Century, seventh edition, 2000

Calibre: 7.62 mm (0.300 in)
Chambering: 0.30 M1906 ('30-06'), rimless
Operation: automatic; short recoil
Locking system: vertically moving block beneath the bolt
Length: 978 mm (38.5 in)
Weight: 15.0 kg (38.5 lb)
Barrel: 610 mm (24.0 in), four grooves, right-hand twist
Mount: tripod
Feed system: fabric belt, 250 rounds
Muzzle velocity: 853 m/sec (2,800 ft/sec) with standard ball ammunition
Cyclic rate: 500 rds/min

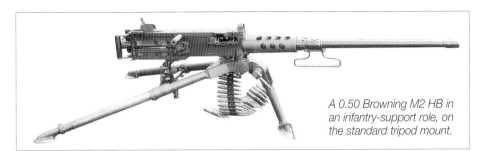

A 0.50 Browning M2 HB in an infantry-support role, on the standard tripod mount.

0.50-calibre guns

The unexpected appearance of the hard-hitting 13mm-calibre German M1918 anti-tank rifle caused General Pershing – commanding the AEF – to call for a machine-gun developing comparable power. After Winchester had tried and failed to provide a suitable cartridge, Frankford Arsenal produced a 0.50 design simply by enlarging the 0.30 M1906 in May 1919.

John Browning had already enlarged the 0.30 M1917 machine-gun to chamber the 0.50 Winchester cartridge, but Frankford Arsenal had developed such a powerful alternative that a hydraulic buffer had to be included in the gun design.

M1921. This was standardised in 1922, though lack of funds deferred purchases until 1925. Only 1,000 guns had been acquired by 1934.

M1921A1 (1930). An important improvement occurred when a compound charging handle replaced the earlier simple radial pattern, easing the strain of cocking the powerful mainspring. This new handle was subsequently fitted to all M1921 guns when they came in for overhaul or repair. The M1921A1 Browning was a great success, permitting an awesome volume of fire to be sustained for long periods. Barrels often burnt-out at the muzzle, which was due to the use of a water-cooling jacket that stopped several inches short of the muzzle. Many US Navy guns acquired auxiliary jackets to protect their muzzles, but the fault was rectified in the M2.

M2 HB (1933). The left-side feed of the M1921 was inappropriate, and so a convertible feed system was developed for the succeeding M1923 and M1923E1, An air-cooled gun was eventually developed from the M1923E1 at the request of the Cavalry Board and was adopted as the 'Caliber .50 Browning Machine Gun, Heavy Barrel, M2'. The finned barrels of the prototypes were abandoned before series production began, and the barrel length was increased in 1938 from 914 mm (36 in) to 1143 mm (45 in), providentially slowing the cyclic rate and improving accuracy. Older guns were modified as they returned for repair. Aircraft guns could be used on ground mounts as long as care was taken not to sustain fire for more than a few minutes at a time.

All M2 Brownings had convertible feed, but almost always fed from the left when used on the standard tripods. Mounts included the Tripods M1921 and M2; the Anti-aircraft Tripods M2, M3 and M43 (or navy Mk 21); the Elevator Cradle M1; and the Anti-aircraft Mount M63 in addition to a collection of multiple vehicle mounts.

M2 (water-cooled). Developed to replace the M1921A1, this had a water jacket that extended past the muzzle to overcome burn-out tendencies. Series-production guns had spade grips if they were used on the ground or on flexible mounts in aircraft, but not if they were to be fixed in vehicles or aircraft. Production of air-cooled M2 machine-guns during the Second World War totalled about 425,000. Others were converted after 1945 from survivors of the 82,500 water-cooled guns.

M3. Attempts began in 1939 to increase the cyclic rate of the standard M2 (800 rds/min) and finally led to the greatly modified M3 (1,200 rds/min) in 1944. Though the M3 was superficially identical with the M2, few parts would interchange.

Browning Automatic Rifle ('BAR')

On the same day that Browning first demonstrated his water-cooled medium machine-gun to the Machine Gun Board, an automatic rifle prototype passed a flawless test and was ordered into immediate mass production. Browning completed development work in collaboration with Colt's Patent Fire Arms Manufacturing Company, while Winchester was made responsible for developing the manufacturing techniques.

The first gas-operated air cooled Browning rifle was completed in February 1918; by Armistice Day, Colt, Winchester, Marlin-Rockwell and their subcontractors had completed 52,000. Production ran on into 1919 and the final total amounted to more than 100,000. However, only a few thousand had reached the Western Front, where they first saw action merely 10 weeks before the fighting ceased.

The Browning was seen as a squad semi-automatic weapon, with its automatic capacity held in reserve. In practice, however, the selector switch was always set for rapid fire, partly to prevent fumbling for the catch and partly because the cyclic rate was slow enough for an experienced man to fire short bursts or even single shots. The Browning also lacked a readily exchangeable barrel.

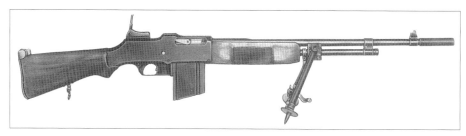

The M1918A1 Browning Automatic Rifle.

M1918A1. The US Army subsequently adapted the M1918 by improving the gas system, adding a bipod and fitting a shoulder rest on top of the butt, but this expedient, lacking the heavy barrel of the M1922, was never ideal for the fire-support role.

M1918A2. The design of the BAR was advanced from 'A1' to 'A2' standards by fitting a modified bipod and shoulder rest, a useless monopod under the butt (almost immediately discarded), and a rate-reducing buffer giving slow (350 rds/min) or rapid (500 rds/min) automatic fire. Several different fore-ends were developed in an attempt to prevent the barrel (which rapidly overheated in rapid fire) from charring the woodwork, but the problem was never solved even though 188,380 M1918A1 rifles were converted to M1918A2 standards during the Second World War.

M1922. Though the Browning Automatic Rifle had performed impressively during the closing stages of the First World War, combat experience had convinced some observers that improvements could be made. Immediately after the Armistice, therefore, the Cavalry Board added a finned barrel and a tripod to permit the rifle to deliver a greater volume of sustained fire before overheating. Designated .30 M1922, only 470 new guns were acquired.

Others. Many BAR-type weapons were sold to law-enforcement agencies, as the Colt Automatic Machine Rifles R-75 and R-80 (also known as the 'Monitor'), and the basic design was also made in Europe – most notably by Fabrique

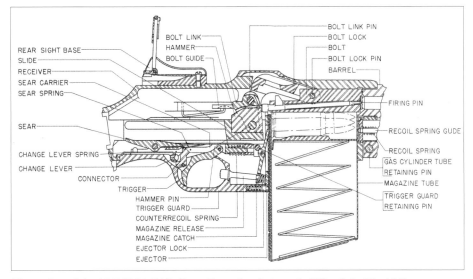

The action of the M1918A1 BAR. From Browning Automatic Rifle, Cal. .30, *All Types (TM 9-122, 1942).*

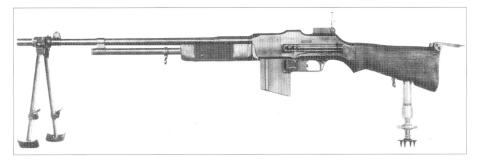

Easily distinguished by the monopod beneath the butt, this is the Colt-made M1918A2 BAR.

Nationale d'Armes de Guerre in Belgium. BAR-type machine rifles were adopted by the armies of Belgium, Poland and Sweden.

Designation: Browning Machine Rifle, Caliber .30, Model 1918A1
Made by Colt's Patent Fire Arms Mfg Co., Hartford, Connecticut, USA, and others (see text)

Specification: Standard pattern
Data taken from Ian Hogg and John Weeks, Military Small Arms of the Twentieth Century, seventh edition, 2000
Calibre: 7.62 mm (0.300 in)
Chambering: 0.30 M1906 ('30-06'), rimless
Operation: selective; gas
Locking system: tilting block engaging the roof of the receiver
Length: 1,219 mm (48.0 in)
Weight: 8.3 kg (18.3 lb) with mount, but no magazine
Barrel: 610 mm (24.0 in), four grooves, right-hand twist
Mount: bipod
Feed system: detachable box, 20 rounds
Muzzle velocity: 807 m/sec (2,650 ft/sec) with standard ball ammunition
Cyclic rate: 500 rds/min

Johnson M1941 and M1944

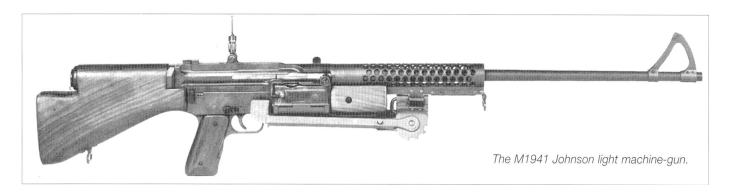

The M1941 Johnson light machine-gun.

Designed in 1937–8 by one of the most controversial figures in US machine-gun history, Melvin M. Johnson, this gun arrived too late for inclusion in military trials undertaken in September 1941. However, Johnson's reputation as a designer (and possibly also his status as a reserve officer in the Marine Corps) persuaded the authorities to undertake special tests later in the same year.

As the specification had called for belt-feed and as it proved to have only marginal reserves of power in adverse conditions, the Johnson was rejected. Yet some of the individual testers thought very highly of it, and a trial undertaken by the Infantry Board at Fort Benning was enthusiastic. Though

Johnson claimed to have sold 10,000 machine-guns to the Dutch East Indies army, the Japanese invaded before large-scale deliveries could be made. The US Army remained sceptical of the value of the M1941, although 125 guns were issued to the First Special Service Force in Italy.

Others were used in the Pacific by the Marines, including the First Marine Parachute Battalion, the consensus being that the handiness of the Johnson M1941 (known commercially as the 'Type H') was a great advantage, as it weighed only 12.8lb. The protrusion of the side-mounted magazine was not particularly popular, even though it could be replenished through the open action

with single rounds or from standard 5-round chargers. This was Johnson's overly optimistic way of overcoming the sustained-fire capability demanded in the original army specifications.

The M1941 had a distinctive appearance, with the return-spring housing continuing back above the wooden butt and a bipod that folded down beneath the fore-end. The straight-line design, which undoubtedly made the gun easier to control that the Browning Automatic Rifle, required folding sights that were easily damaged. Most guns fired from a closed breech when firing single shots, but from an open breech when firing automatically to prevent a chambered round 'cooking off'.

Model 1944. The failure of the M1941 to attract large army orders persuaded Johnson to draw attention to his case publicly, which he did with great panache but comparatively little success. Towards the end of the war, he submitted an improved M1941 with a modified selective-fire action, a tubular butt sheathed in plastic, and a monopod beneath the fore-end. The first trials were disappointing, and the prototype passed its acceptance trial only after extensive modifications had been made. Ten were ordered for a large-scale trial, but were not delivered until after hostilities in Europe had ended. The Johnson Automatics Trust subsequently sold the M1944 production rights to Israel in the late 1940s, where guns were made under the name 'Dror'.

Para Model. This was a short-barrelled version of the M1944, offered with a 508 mm (20 in) barrel, reducing overall length to 1,029 mm (40.5 in) and weight by a few ounces. Designed to dismantle into pouches, it was made only in prototype form.

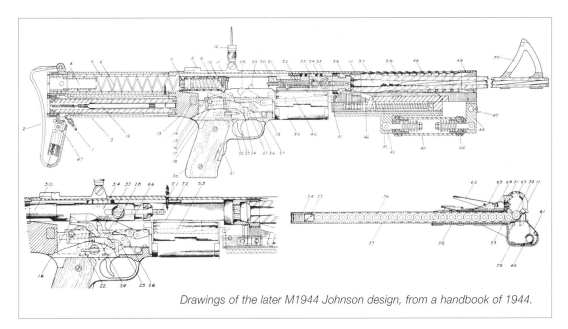

Drawings of the later M1944 Johnson design, from a handbook of 1944.

Designation: Johnson Machine Gun, Caliber 0.30-inch, Model of 1944
Made by Johnson Automatics Mfg Co., Providence, Rhode Island, USA

Specification: Standard 1944 pattern
Data taken from The Model 1944 Johnson Light Machine Gun or Light Rifle, 1945
Calibre: 7.62 mm (0.300 in)
Chambering: 0.30 M1906 ('30-06')
Operation: selective; short recoil
Locking system: rotating multi-lug bolt

Length: 1,067 mm (42.0 in)
Weight: 6.7 kg (14.7 lb) including mount
Barrel: 559 mm (22.0 in), four grooves, right-hand twist
Mount: bipod, 770 gm (1.7 lb)
Feed system: detachable box magazine, 20 rounds, plus five rounds in the feed-way
Muzzle velocity: 805 m/sec (2,640 ft/sec) with standard ball ammunition
Cyclic rate: 600 rds/min, dependent on spring and buffer design

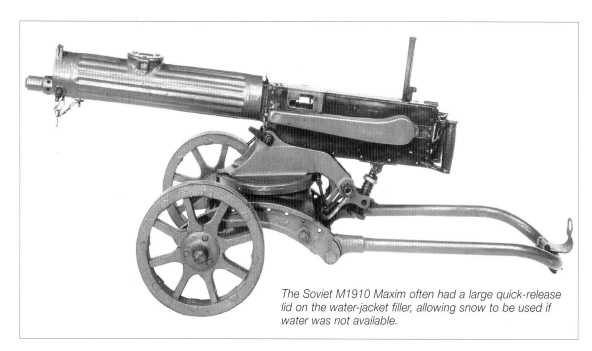

The Soviet M1910 Maxim often had a large quick-release lid on the water-jacket filler, allowing snow to be used if water was not available.

The old Russian Maxims (see above) served on into the Civil War, and then with the Red Army. An attempt had also been made in this period to modify the Maxim design to fire a 13 mm round, but this also proved unsuccessful and few of these weapons were ever made, the

only recorded delivery being that of eight to military educational establishments in the Moscow area.

In 1931, however, the design was upgraded; the water jacket was strengthened to increase rigidity, changes were made to the back plate,

a safety catch was added, the fusee spring gained a tension indicator, and the trigger mechanism was improved. A Vladimirov universal mount, which could be converted instantly to an anti-aircraft tripod, was introduced in 1931, but was too heavy to gain widespread acceptance.

Shortly after the German invasion of the USSR in the summer of 1941, the Tula design bureau simplified the Maxim to make it easier to make. Credited to Lubenets and Karazin, the changes included simplified back sights, the omission of the optical-sight bracket on guns intended for infantry service, and the replacements of the original machined-steel feed block with an aluminium-alloy casting. The most obvious change, however, was the large-diameter filling cap on the water jacket, with a quick-release catch. Experience in the war with Finland (1940–1) had shown the desirability of filing the jacket with snow if water could not be found.

By 1945, a variety of non-standard guns had also been pressed into service. These included damaged water-cooled guns, which had been converted by cutting cooling slots in the jackets, and a variety of cannibalised guns assembled in Leningrad during the siege. The latter could be old ex-Tsarist guns, or mixtures of Tsarist and Soviet parts. They often had crudely made armoured shields, and simple disc-type wheels.

Production of the PM continued virtually until the end of the war, though gradually declining in 1944–5 in favour of the SG-43. Consequently, the Russian Maxims were made in substantial numbers; though the cumulative totals are unknown, more than 55,000 guns were made in 1942 alone.

Makim-Tokarev. The first attempts to provide a lightened air-cooled Maxim were taken in 1923, and a committee was formed in September 1924 to oversee work. A Kolesnikov prototype was readied for trial in the summer of 1924 and a Tokarev design followed in November. A few guns of each type were made in the Tula ordnance factory,

but the Tokarev was declared preferable in May 1925. Field trials showed it to be heavy, badly balanced, awkward to carry, and prone to jamming, but the Maxim-Tokarev or 'MT' was ordered into series production. Tula made 2,450 of them in 1926–7. Persistent problems sent the designer back to the drawing board, but the improved gun proffered in 1927 had lost so much commonality with the PM that the entire project was abandoned. Most of the survivors were sent to Spain during the Civil War (1936–9), though a few, perhaps originally dispatched to the Russo-Japanese border, ended their days in China.

PV-1. Also known as the 'Maxim-Nadashkevich' or M1928, this was developed in the Aviaworker and Tula factories in 1923-6. It could be identified by its lightweight barrel and slotted sheet-steel barrel casing, and by the use of a metallic-link belt instead of the fabric patterns associated with the PM. A conical sleeve-type muzzle booster raised the cyclic rate to about 750 rds/min, and a spring-buffer smoothed the transmission of recoil forces to the mount. Some guns were fitted with synchronisers, but others were mounted in the wings away from the propeller disc. The first guns fed ammunition from the left, but a right-hand feed was approved in December 1929 to permit

double-gun installations. The PV-1 was made from 1926 until 1939, though annual production rarely exceeded 3,000. The length of the barrel was increased in the summer of 1930 to standardise with the PM.

Designation 'Pulemet Maxima, obraztsa 1910 goda'
Made by Tula ordnance factory and, apparently, the Kovrov machine-gun factory

Specification: Standard M1910
Data taken from A. J. Barker and John Walter, Russian Infantry Weapons of World War II, 1971
Calibre: 7.62 mm (0.300 in)
Chambering: 7.62 x 54 mm, rimmed
Operation: automatic; short recoil with gas boost
Locking system: multi-part toggle, breaking downward
Length: 1,107 mm (43.6 in)
Weight: of gun 23.8 kg (52.5 lb) without mount
Barrel: 721 mm (28.4 in), four grooves, right-hand twist
Mount: Sokolov carriage (45.2 kg/99.6 lb) or Kolesnikov tripod
Feed system: fabric belt, 250 rounds
Muzzle velocity: 863 m/sec (2,830 ft/sec) with Type L ball ammunition
Cyclic rate: 550 rds/min

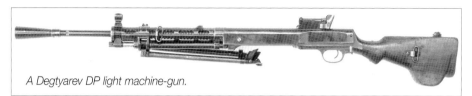

A Degtyarev DP light machine-gun.

This was the first new machine-gun design to be standardised in the Red Army, replacing a variety of guns, derived from the Fedorov automatic rifle ('AVF'), that had included variants fed from Lewis-type pan magazines and others that had two or even three barrels. The work of Vasiliy Alexeyevich Degtyarev, based on designs that had originated in the early 1920s, the prototype DP was submitted for trials in September 1926. The gun worked well enough to demonstrate its potential, but many parts broke and the mechanism was subject to frequent jamming. A process of improvement began, aiming at a jam rate of 1 round in 200, but the action was judged to be too violent until the gas port had been moved forward. In 1927, however, the DP ('P' for Pekhotniy, 'infantry') trounced the Maxim-Tokarev and the German Dreyse in comparative trials.

The DP was adopted provisionally in March 1927 and ordered into series production even before trials had been completed. The basic design was eventually refined until it became acceptably reliable, though inherent problems remained. One of the worst was the position of the return spring, beneath the barrel where it proved to be susceptible to heat. Soviet spring-making technology was not particularly good in this era, but it took the authorities until 1944 to move the spring to the rear of the receiver. Ironically, an experimental gun tested in 1931 already included this modification. However, the army continued to experiment with modifications to the DP and came close to adopting a Japanese-type hopper magazine in 1938.

The DP, a gas-operated weapon working on the Kjellman-Friberg locking system, was the standard light machine gun of the Soviet forces until the introduction of the DPM. It is easily recognised by the pan magazine that, although undoubtedly inspired by the Lewis pattern, has a fixed outer casing; only the inner centre revolves around the spindle.

The butt has a shallow pistol grip stock and a slotted stamped-steel casing protects the finned barrel. A detachable bipod is fixed around the gas tunnel, but was the source of widespread complaints. A stronger non-detachable bipod was substituted in later designs. A grip safety lies behind the trigger guard.

The unaltered DP served throughout the Second World War, huge quantities being made. It could be recognised by the design of the butt, with a shallow pistol grip and a grip safety system; the later DPM had a separate pistol grip.

DA. Adopted in 1929, this was the basic Degtyarev aircraft gun. It had a lightweight barrel, lacked the barrel casing, and had a plate in front of the receiver to accept the pintle mount and the ring-type back sight. The design of the gas cylinder had to be altered to accept the plate. A rubber-covered handle replaced the butt of the infantry machine-gun, and a pistol grip was riveted (welded on later guns) to the rear receiver bracket. The change in layout made the grip safety system redundant, to be replaced by a manual lever on the receiver. The DA-2 (1930) was a two-barrelled version of the DA, adopted officially but made only in small numbers. The calibre was too small to be effective and the pan magazines were cumbersome.

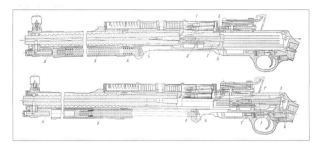

Drawings of the action of the Degtyarev. From Federov's Evolyutsiya Strelkovogo Oruzhiya (1938).

DT. The prototype of this tank and vehicle gun, developed by Georgiy Shpagin, was readied for trial in August 1928. The most obvious features were a telescoping steel butt, a wooden pistol grip, an aperture sight on the receiver (400–1,000 m), and the ball mount. The barrel lacked the slotted sheet-steel casing of the DP. However, the DT could be dismounted to serve as a ground-defence gun once a bipod and a front sight carried aboard the vehicle had been attached. The pan magazines held 60 rounds in two tiers. A separate optical sight was often used in tank and vehicle mounts.

DPM (Degtyareva pekhotniy modernizirovanniy, 'Degtyarev infantry, modernised'). Approved in August 1944 as a result of complaints about the performance of the DP, this exhibited several major improvements made by Degtyarev, Belyaev and Skvortsov. The fragile detachable bipod of the DP had been replaced by a sturdier fixed pattern, the bipod clamp of the DPM being attached to the barrel casing rather than to the gas tunnel beneath; the DPM was permitted to revolve around the axis of the barrel to permit levelling the weapon on uneven terrain. The return spring was moved to a cylindrical extension projecting from the rear of the receiver, a manual safety replaced the grip safety lever of the DP, and a pistol grip was added to the stock. The weapon first reached the Soviet troops in October 1944, soon proving itself to be more accurate and reliable than the preceding DP.

DTM. This was modified from the improved DPM infantry weapon. Fitted with a retractable steel stock and a 60-round pan magazine, it was virtually identical to the DT except for the positioning of the recoil spring cylinder at the rear of the receiver.

Designation: Pulemet Degtyareva pekhotniy, obraztsa 1927 goda ('DP obr. 1927g')
Made by Tula ordnance factory, and possibly also in Kovrov

Specification: Standard infantry gun
Data taken from V. G. Fedorov, Evolyutsiya Strelkovogo Oruzhiya – II. Razvitie avtomaticheskogo oruzhiya, 1938
Calibre: 7.62 mm (0.300 in)
Chambering: 7.62 x 54mm, rimmed
Operation: automatic; gas
Locking system: flaps on the bolt engaging the receiver walls
Length*: 1,266 mm (49.8 in)
Weight of gun: 7.77 kg (17.1 lb) without magazine
Barrel: 605 mm (23.8 in), four grooves, right-hand twist
Mount: bipod
Feed system: detachable pan, 47 rounds
Muzzle velocity: 848 m/sec (2,780 ft/sec) with standard Type L ball ammunition
Cyclic rate: 600 rds/min

The DTM was a tank and vehicle gun, introduced in 1944. The tube extending from the back of the receiver contains the return spring that had previously been under the barrel.

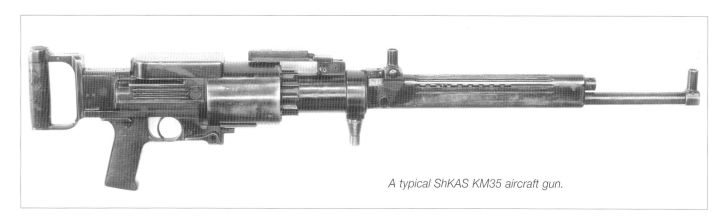

A typical ShKAS KM35 aircraft gun.

Designed by Boris Shpitalniy and Irnahr Komaritskiy, this was developed to provide an aircraft gun with a rate of fire that was substantially greater than that of the KV-1 or the DA. The prototype was submitted in 1930, and after successfully completing its trials, seven guns were ordered in February 1932. The 'M1932' was adopted in October 1932, but the ShKAS was still a long way from perfection. A revised prototype was submitted early in 1933 and series assembly of KM-33 guns had begun by 1934.

However, experience soon showed that the ShKAS still needed improvement.

The difficulties arose not so much from the complexity of action, but from the design and quality of the springs. Individual guns could fire at rates as high as 2,000 rds/min, generating so much heat that the original springs frequently failed after only a few minutes. A solution was eventually found in the development of multi-strand springs, which extended operating life considerably.

The perfected KM-35 was intended for ring mounts, but a few were adapted to mount in the wings. These lacked charging handles, and were operated by cables. A synchronised version (KM-36) was approved in 1936. ShKAS machine-

guns were occasionally pressed into ground service, usually on anti-aircraft mounts, though it has been claimed that a few were given bipods to serve in 'last-ditch' defensive positions. The fire-rate was so high that they must have been exceptionally difficult to control in any infantry role.

ShKAS machine-guns had a unique feed system, often known as the 'squirrel cage', which supported the belt while a round was taken from the belt, chambered, fired, extracted, and ejected in two stages. The action was so smooth and efficient that the Soviet authorities developed an 'Ultra ShKAS' capable of firing 2,800–3,000 rds/min. However, all the guns were sensitive to variations in ammunition. They were supposed to be fired exclusively with special rounds, distinguished by the character 'Ш' ('Sh') in the headstamp. The bullets were crimped into the case-mouths and special attention was paid to securing the primers.

It has been suggested that the ShKAS never reached series production, requiring too much handwork to be made in anything other than small batches. However, Soviet production figures show that more than 73,000 of them were made in the Tula ordnance factory in 1933–40.

ShVAK. This was an enlargement of the basic design, lacking the special feed. A prototype was tested as early as 1932, but priorities were allocated elsewhere and not until the end of 1934 did work recommence. The 12.7 mm machine-gun was adopted in 1935 and made in comparatively small numbers until replaced by the Berezin design in 1941. It also provided the basis for the exceptionally successful 20 mm ShVAK cannon, which remained in production until the end of the war.

Designation: Shpitalniy-Komariskiy aviatsionniy skorostrelniy pulemet obraztsa 1935 goda ('ShKAS M1935') Made by Tula ordnance factory

Specification: Standard KM35
Data taken from D. N. Bolotin, Soviet Small Arms and Ammunition (1995), and others; * marks approximate dimensions
Calibre: 7.62 mm (0.300 in)
Chambering: 7.62 x 54 mm, rimmed
Operation: automatic; gas
Locking system: displacement of the bolt
Length: 1,000 mm (39.4 in)*
Weight: of gun 10.5 kg (23.1 lb)
Barrel: 605 mm (23.8 in),* four grooves, right-hand twist
Mount: ring or turret
Feed system: disintegrating-link belt, 250 rounds
Muzzle velocity: 800 m/sec (2,625 ft/sec) with standard ball ammunition
Cyclic rate: 1800 rds/min

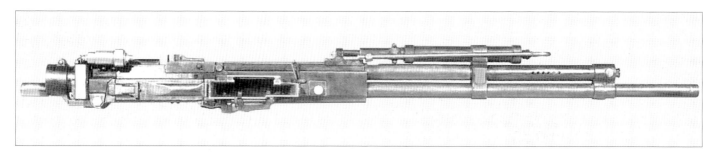

The 12.7 mm UB or Berezin aircraft gun. This is the 'K' or wing-mounted pattern with a pneumatic charging mechanism.

Designed by Mikhail Berezin, this resulted from a competition to find a 12.7 mm machine-gun that was suitable for synchronisation, but was simpler and easier to make than the ShVAK. Locked by a sliding wedge, a prototype was successfully tested in October 1938 and had soon demonstrated its potential. Series production of the 'BS' was ordered in April 1939, but progress was slow and field trials were not undertaken until the first months of 1941. These revealed that some of the parts were too weak to withstand a constant battering, and that the charging stroke was too hard.

A modified pattern ('UB') was adopted in April 1941 for universal service, but series production did not begin in earnest

until after the German invasion. The Berezin was made in three patterns: the UBK and the synchroniser-compatible UBS were mounted in aircraft wings, being charged pneumatically, and the UBK was a ring-mounted observer's gun that could be charged manually.

Output has been estimated as 125,000 guns in 1943–5. Just as the 7.62 mm ShKAS became the 12.7 mm and 20 mm ShVAK, so the 12.7mm-calibre Beresin was altered to produce the compact and exceptionally successful B-20 20 mm cannon.

Designation: Pulemet universalniy Berezina ('UB')
Manufacturer unknown (Kovrov machine-gun factory?)

Specification: Standard UBS
Data taken from D. N. Bolotin, Soviet Small Arms and Ammunition, 1995, and others; * marks approximate dimensions
Calibre: 12.7 mm (0.500 in)
Chambering: 12.7 x 108 mm, rimless
Operation: automatic; gas
Locking system: separate locking wedge engaging the bolt
Length: 1,620 mm (63.75 in)*
Weight of gun: 21.45 kg (23.6 lb)
Barrel: 935 mm (36.8 in),* four grooves, right-hand twist
Mount: ring or turret
Feed system: disintegrating-link belt, 250 rounds
Muzzle velocity: 830 m/sec (ft/sec) with standard ball ammunition
Cyclic rate: 700–800 rds/min

Soviet women armourers replenish the ammunition supply of a 12.7mm Berezin UB, mounted as an observer's gun in the rear of the cockpit of an Ilyushin Il-2M3 Stormovik ground-attack aircraft.

Degtyarev-Shpagin M1938 ('DShK') USSR

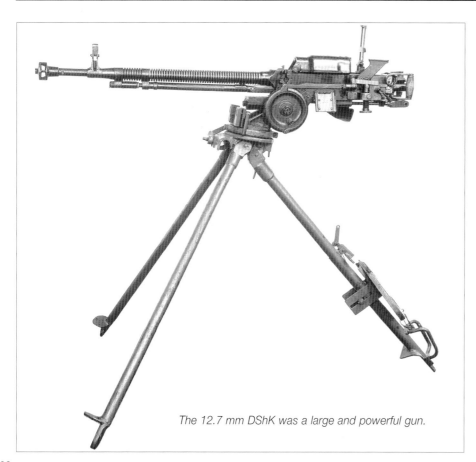

The 12.7 mm DShK was a large and powerful gun.

By 1930, the first attempts had been made to modify the Degtyarev light machine-gun to fire a 12.7 mm cartridge suited to a heavy support role. An experimental Degtyarev design was tested against a Tula-made Dreyse in 1931, performing satisfactorily enough for a batch of 'DK' machine-guns to be ordered in 1933. However, the low cyclic rate and cumbersome drum magazines were unacceptable, and although more guns were made to allow trials to continue, work stopped in 1935.

An 'open cylinder' feed credited to Georgiy Shpagin was then added, based on a rotary block above the receiver, protected by a stamped-steel shroud, that stripped cartridges from the links in the metal-link belt, revolved them around the block and indexed them into the chamber. The goal was to provide a feed that allied the certainty and uniformity of a drum with the capacity of a belt. The cyclic rate was also increased.

The resulting DShK was adopted in February 1939. The first series-production guns reached the troops in 1940, and the DShK remained in service throughout the war. It was also used as the secondary armament on some of the larger armoured vehicles and on a number of the smaller naval patrol vessels.

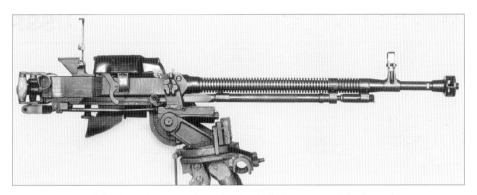

This view of the DShK clearly shows how the feed block, on top of the breech, was protected by a stamped-steel cover. The forked indexing lever was operated by the base of the charging handle.

The locking mechanism was that of the standard Degtyarev infantry machine-gun, the DP1928, which cammed the bolt unit flaps in and out of the receiver walls. The external appearance of the DShK resembled that of the DS, with spade grips, the trigger unit mounted on the backplate, a barrel with cooling fins and a large muzzle brake/compensator welded to the muzzle.

A standard pattern of leaf rear sight was normally fitted, but this was occasionally replaced by the M1938, M1941 or M1942 anti-aircraft sights. A dual purpose ground and anti-aircraft mount was provided and two small wheels were issued to enable the unit to be easily moved; to convert this for AA

fire, the wheels were removed and the trail extended to form a shoulder high tripod. An armoured shield was often provided, and the guns were occasionally used in double or quadruple anti-aircraft mounts. Production was initially slow, amounting to no more than 2,000 prior to the German invasion, but was accelerated rapidly. Only 720 guns were reportedly in the hands of combat units in January 1942, but the total had climbed to more than 8,000 by January 1944.

DShKM. This was an improved from of the DShK, credited to Sokolov and Norov, with a bi-directional feed adapted for disintegrating-link belts. Some of the parts were stamped, the method of attaching the barrel to the receiver was

improved, and a rebound suppressor was added. It is usually claimed that the changes were made after the war (leading to the designation 'DShKM 38/46'), but the first batches were made in Saratov in February 1945 and undoubtedly saw combat.

Designation: Pulemet Degtyareva-Shpagina Krupnokaliberniy, obraztsa 1938 goda ('DShK M1938')
Made by Tula ordnance factory and elsewhere

Specification: Standard infantry pattern
Data taken from A. J. Barker and John Walter, Russian Infantry Weapons of World War II, 1971
Calibre: 12.7 mm (0.500 in)
Chambering: 12.7 x 108, rimless
Operation: automatic; gas
Locking system: flaps in the bolt engaging recesses in the receiver walls
Length: 1,602 mm (62.3 in)
Weight of gun: 33.3 kg (73.5 lb)
Barrel: 1002 mm (39.4 in), four grooves, right-hand twist?
Mount: tripod, 142 kg/313 lb without auxiliary wheels
Feed system: metal-link belt, 50 or 250 rounds
Muzzle velocity: 843 m/sec (2,765 ft/sec) with standard ball ammunition
Cyclic rate: 580 rds/min

Degtyarev M1939 ('DS') USSR

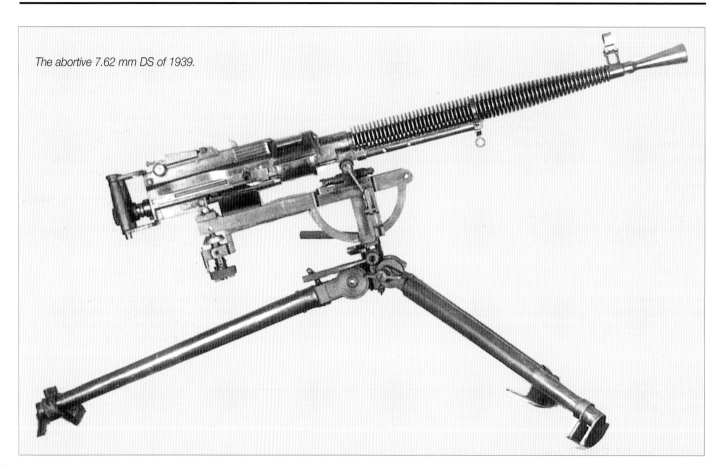

The abortive 7.62 mm DS of 1939.

This ill-fated design had a lengthy pedigree, dating back to trials undertaken in 1930. An adaptation of the DP, with a rotary feed-block credited to Shpagin, the experimental guns were adapted to feed Maxim-type fabric belts in 1933, relying on studs on the bolt to pull the cartridges backward from the belt and a lever on the receiver cover to lower them in line with the feed pawls. The guns fed from the right and ejected downward. Tests undertaken in 1934–8 suggested a variety of improvements, and a variable fire-rate mechanism was added. The higher rate (1,100 rpm) was considered more suitable for anti-aircraft work, and the lower (550 rpm) for the ground role: the rate of fire could be altered simply by changing the size of the gas port aperture and altering the tension in the buffer spring. The original pistol grip was replaced by spade grips and a replaceable barrel was provided, A convertible, dual purpose, wheeled tripod mount – sometimes shielded – was generally used with this weapon in the infantry role.

The gun was officially adopted in September 1939. Tooling in the Tula factory began immediately and the first guns were assembled in June 1940, largely because work on the Maxim had been greatly reduced.

The DS was light and manoeuvrable, but service showed that it also had many faults. It was prone to ignite cartridges before the action was locked, had a violent feed stroke, broke components regularly, and was unreliable in cold or dusty conditions. Remedial work proved to be impossible, and the invasion of the Soviet Union by the Germans in June 1941 forced the reinstatement of the Maxim.

The DS was abandoned after only about 10,300 had been made. Degtyarev continued work on the basic design, refining it to a point where it worked efficiently, but the GVG (the prototype SG) proved to be more reliable and potentially easier to make.

Designation: Pulemet Degtyareva stankoviy ('DS')
Made by Tula ordnance factory

Specification: Standard gun
Data taken from A. J. Barker and John Walter, Russian Infantry Weapons of World War II, 1971, and D. N. Bolotin, Soviet Small Arms and Ammunition, 1995
Calibre: 7.62 mm (0.300 in)
Chambering: 7.62 x 54 mm, rimmed
Operation: automatic; gas
Locking system: flaps on the bolt engaging the receiver walls
Length: 1,171 mm (46.1 in)
Weight of gun: 14.3 kg (31.5 lb) without mount
Barrel: 721 mm (28.4 in), four grooves, right-hand twist
Mount: tripod
Feed system: fabric belt, 50 or 250 rounds
Muzzle velocity: 860 m/sec (2,820 ft/sec) with standard ball ammunition
Cyclic rate: 600 or 1,200 rds/min (selectable)

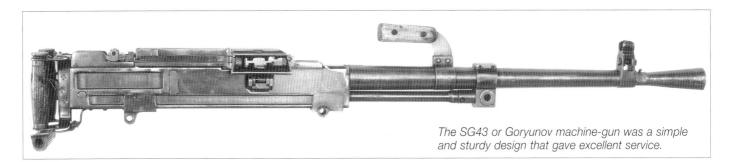

The SG43 or Goryunov machine-gun was a simple and sturdy design that gave excellent service.

The design of a talented engineer named Petr Goryunov, this dated back to 1938. A prototype had been tested successfully in June 1941, but not until a competition was held in May 1942 did the GVG (as the Goryunov gun was then known) demonstrate its superiority. A batch of 50 guns had been made by March 1943. Tests were favourable, but suggested changes that should be made. A carrying handle was added to the barrel, making changing easier; the feed was changed from right to left; the feed block was machined from a forging instead of stamped from sheet steel; a leaf sight replaced the original tangent-leaf type; and the tripod mount was altered to accept wheels. After negotiating field trials, the improved

GVG was officially adopted in May 1943 as the 'SG' (or 'SG-43') – but only after Degtyarev, whom Stalin favoured, admitted that the GVG was more reliable than his perfected DS and an easier mass-production proposition. Petr Goryunov died in 1943 after a period of ill-health, and much of the development work had been undertaken by his collaborators, nephew Mikhail Goryunov and an engineer named Voronkov.

For the first time since the Maxim, the Russians departed from the Degtyarev flap-lock and turned instead to a system that cammed the rear of the bolt into the right side of the receiver wall. The SG was a slender weapon with spade grips and the trigger unit mounted on the back plate. The barrel lacked cooling fins, but

had a prominent flash-hider and a folding carrying handle. The standard mount was a dual purpose ground/anti-aircraft mounting, equipped with wheels to facilitate movement.

Combat soon showed that the SG was an excellent weapon, and it rapidly gained popularity as production accelerated. The connection between the barrel and the receiver was found to be poor, and some of the components of the trigger system needed strengthening. The result was the SGM, introduced in 1945. The modified pattern can usually be identified by fluting in the barrel surface, which saved weight without sacrificing rigidity, and significantly increased the surface area presented to the atmosphere.

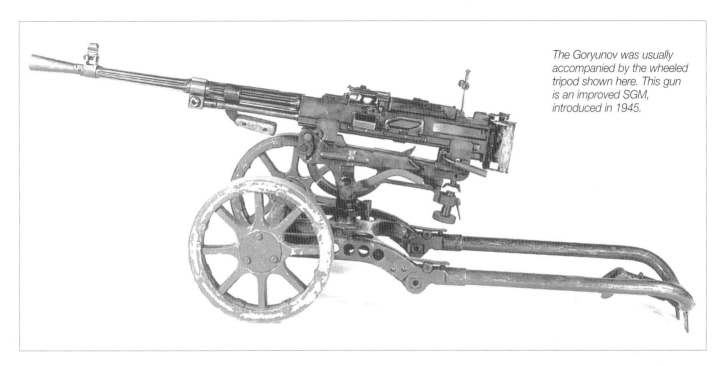

The Goryunov was usually accompanied by the wheeled tripod shown here. This gun is an improved SGM, introduced in 1945.

Designation: Pulemet stankoviy
Goryunova, obraztsa 1943 goda
('SG-43')
Made by Kovrov machine-gun factory,
and possibly also in Tula

Specification: Standard infantry pattern
Data taken from A. J. Barker and
John Walter, Russian Infantry
Weapons of World War II, 1971

Calibre: 7.62 mm (0.300 in)
Chambering: 7.62 x 54 mm, rimmed
Operation: automatic; gas
Locking system: displacement of the
bolt-tail into the receiver wall
Length: 1,120 mm (44.1 in)
Weight of gun: 13.8 kg (30.4 lb) without
mount
Barrel: 719 mm (28.3 in), four grooves,
right-hand twist

Mount: wheeled tripod (26.9 kg/59.3 lb)
Feed system: fabric or metal-link belt,
250 rounds
Muzzle velocity: 855 m/sec (2,805
ft/sec) with standard ball ammunition
Cyclic rate: 600 rds/min

Appendix: Lesser guns

This material contains details that show the confusion that could arise from the issue of captured weapons. Like the body of the book, it concentrates on the weapons of the belligerents in the two World Wars.

Belgium

- The Belgian infantry weapon was the Maxim, many of which were captured (and used) by the Germans in 1914. The Belgians had experimented with the Berthier machine rifle and then adopted the Lewis Gun prior to the First World War, the latter, chambering 7.65 x 53 rimless cartridges, being made for Armes Automatiques Lewis by BSA. Few had been supplied by 1914, however, and the Belgians appear to have used Hotchkiss and other French weapons during the war.
- From the 1920s onwards, Fabrique Nationale d'Armes de Guerre made large quantities of Browning machine guns and Browning-type automatic rifles, known commercially as the 'M1930' and 'Model D'. The rifles were widely exported in a variety of chamberings.

Britain

- Among the Lewis Guns supplied under Lend-Lease were 1157 0.30 M1917 Lewis ground guns and 38,040 0.30 M1918 aircraft guns. They generally had broad red bands around the barrels or barrel casings to indicate chambers for American .30 cartridges instead of the British 0.303. Half the pan-magazine disc was also originally painted red. Enfield transformed about 15,000 American aircraft guns in 1940 and Parker-Hale adapted at least 1,000 in 1941.

- About 10,000 0.30 M1917 water-cooled Browning medium machine-guns were also supplied under Lend-Lease; 16,500 additional 0.30 Brownings were purchased from the USA and Canada in 1941, together with 722 kits to transform aircraft Brownings into M1919A4 ground guns.

China

- The Chinese government ordered 50 Škoda M1909 machine-guns to accompany field artillery and armour plate. None were delivered owing to 1911 revolution. The standard Chinese infantry-support gun was a Maxim, though the Madsen also appears to have served in some numbers with cavalry units.

Czechoslovakia

- The standard Czech heavy machine-gun had originally been the ex-Austrian Schwarzlose, small quantities of the 07/12 model being converted to 'vz. 07/24' standards (and the 7.92 mm cartridge) by the Janeček factory in Mnichovo Hradiště in 1924–5. New 'vz. 24' guns were also produced for several years, permitting a small export market to be created, but were clearly antiquated.

Germany

- When the Germans invaded Czechoslovakia, they seized existing ZB guns (vz. 26, vz. 30, vz. 30/J, ZGB) and immediately reissued them to the Wehrmacht. Modifications were unnecessary as they already chambered the standard German 7.9 mm service cartridge. Known as 'leichte Maschinengewehre 26 (t) und 30 (t)' in German service, they were greatly favoured by Fallschirmjäger and Waffen-SS.

Work continued for some years after the German invasion, but was then greatly reduced in favour of the MG. 34.

- The Germans also seized ZB vz. 57 (ZB 53) guns, issuing them as 'schwere Maschinengewehre 37 (t)' when production of the MG. 34 was lagging and the MG. 42 had yet to appear. Production was moved from Brno to Vsetin in 1941, but gradually declined as the facilities were put to making parts for the standard German machine-guns. They were generally issued with Czech-made ZB 308 tripods, but may sometimes be encountered adapted for standard German mounts.
- German manuals, and Fischer's Leitfaden für die Ordnungspolizei, suggest that small numbers of the French Saint-Étienne M1907/16 machine-gun and the CSRG ('Chauchat') machine rifle were issued to the police in small numbers. It is suspected that these were restricted to training, or held in reserve.
- A huge variety of Soviet weaponry was captured, particularly in the summer of 1941. These included light and heavy Degtyarev, Maxim and ultimately even Goryunov machine-guns. Many were immediately impressed into service against their former owners.

Japan

- In 1929 guns were purchased from Vickers-Armstrong and issued to the army air service as the 'Type 89 aircraft fixed gun', chambered for the 7.7 mm Type 89 (British 0.303) cartridge. The Type 97 navy aircraft fixed machine-gun was a modified version of the army Type 89, introduced to the naval air service in 1937. Belt-fed and air-cooled, it chambered the 7.7 mm semi-rim Type 92 ammunition. The similar Type 98 heavy machine-gun (which had a water-jacket) was introduced for the Japanese army of occupation in Manchuria in 1938, to overcome a shortage of guns. The Types 97 and 98 were made in Japan.

- Ammunition supply was complicated further when the army air service purchased many Maschinengewehr 15 (MG 15) guns from Rheinmetall-Borsig in Germany; for these chambered the standard rimless German 7.9 mm round, known in Japanese terms as the 7.9 mm Type 98. A few Type 98 army aircraft guns were later used by the infantry on simple bipods.
- The last Japanese machine-guns were copies of the American Browning. The 12.7 mm Type 1 saw widespread service as an aircraft weapon and was mooted as a possible replacement for the Type 93 heavy infantry-support machine-gun. The 7.7 mm Type 1 aircraft gun could well have replaced the 7.7 Type 92 and Type 1 strip-feed ground guns, but few were spared for infantry use. The 13.2 mm Type 3 aircraft gun was developed to take the 13.2 mm Type 93 cartridge, which proved more comparable to the US 0.50 M2 than the inferior short-case 12.7 mm pattern, and the 7.7 mm Type 4 tank machine-gun was planned to replace the Types 91 and 97. Excepting the Type 1 aircraft guns, only a few prototypes and pre-production Brownings were made before the arms industry collapsed in 1945.

The Netherlands

- The principal service weapons were the M1908/13 Schwarzlose and M1920 Lewis Guns. The authorities also purchased substantial quantities of 6.5 mm-calibre Madsen light machine-guns, in a variety of patterns that included some for colonial service with the Netherlands Indies army (KNIL.).

Poland

- The Polish forces were armed largely with German MG. 08 Maxims, obtained after the end of the First World War, though these were supplemented by M1930 water-cooled 1917-type Brownings. However, there were also substantial quantities of BAR-type machine rifles, 10,000 of the latter being ordered from Fabrique Nationale d'Armes de Guerre in December 1927.

Romania

- The Romanian M30 was similar to the Czechoslovakian-made ZB 30/J (developed for Yugoslavia), chambering the same 7.92 mm cartridge; 17,131 were made in Brno and about 10,000 by CMC in Cugir. Small quantities of these weapons eventually entered German service by way of Romanian units serving on the Eastern Front.

Russia

- The Russian cavalry had used the Madsen during the Russo-Japanese War. Though the guns had been withdrawn in 1905, others had been purchased by 1914 and more followed during the First World War. The manufacturer of the Madsen, Dansk Rekyriffel Syndikat, had even been persuaded to build a factory in Kovrov (though this did not become operational until after the 1917 Revolution, making Maxims).

USA

- The British .303 Vickers Gun was adopted as the 0.30 Machine Gun M1915 after trials in April 1916, a production licence was acquired and 125 modified guns were ordered from Britain. The order was increased to 4,000 when the USA entered the First World War in 1917, but the first guns did not reach the American Expeditionary Force until February 1918. Made by Vickers (6,112) and Colt (3,125), the M1915 proved to be an excellent support weapon and was regarded as the front-line machine-gun until the advent of the M1917 Browning.

- Colt also made about 900 Vickers Aircraft Machine Guns M1918, in accordance with a 14,235-gun contract awarded too late to have any effect on the aerial war.
- The Ordnance Department also sanctioned an adaptation of 7.62 mm-calibre Colt-made Vickers guns destined for Tsarist Russia, but retained in Hartford after the October Revolution. These were transformed for the French 11 mm (Gras) cartridge to provide a hard-hitting anti-balloon gun on the Western Front.

Yugoslavia

- Purchased 1500 ZB vz. 26 light machine-guns from Československá Zbrojovka in 1927, followed by 15,500 Z.B. 30/J guns chambering the 7.92 mm infantry-rifle cartridge. Many of these weapons survived to be confiscated by the Germans in 1941.